Principles of Christian Obedience

Principles of Christian Obedience

Charles G. Finney

BETHANY HOUSE PUBLISHERS
MINNEAPOLIS, MINNESOTA 55438
A Division of Bethany Fellowship, Inc.

Published by Bethany House Publishers
A Ministry of Bethany Fellowship, Inc.
6820 Auto Club Road, Minneapolis, Minnesota 55438

Printed in the United States of America

Library of Congress Cataloging-in-Publication Data

Finney, Charles Grandison, 1792–1875.
    Principles of Christian obedience / Charles G. Finney ; compiled
and edited by Louis Gifford Parkhurst, Jr.
        p. cm.
    A collection of 14 sermons published in 1840 in the Oberlin
evangelist.

    1. Obedience—Religious aspects—Christianity—Sermons.
2. Sermons, American. I. Parkhurst, Louis Gifford, 1946–

II. Title.
BV4647.02F56   1990
234'.6—dc20   89–71071
ISBN 1-55661-050-5   CIP

DEDICATION

To Jack Key, who has encouraged me as a pastor, editor and writer, who made resources available to make this series possible: "It is not often that someone comes along who is a true friend and a good writer." Jack is both.

BOOKS IN THIS SERIES

Answers to Prayer
Principles of Christian Obedience
Principles of Devotion
Principles of Discipleship
Principles of Faith
Principles of Holiness
Principles of Liberty
Principles of Love
Principles of Prayer
Principles of Revival
Principles of Salvation
Principles of Sanctification
Principles of Union with Christ
Principles of Victory

OTHER BOOKS BY FINNEY

Finney's Systematic Theology
Heart of Truth, Finney's Outline of Theology
Reflections on Revival
Finney on Revival
Promise of the Spirit
Autobiography of Charles G. Finney
The Believer's Secret of Spiritual Power (with Andrew Murray)

The Life and Ministry of Charles Finney / Lewis Drummond

CHARLES G. FINNEY was one of America's foremost evangelists. Over half a million people were converted under his ministry in an age that offered neither amplifiers nor mass communication as tools. Harvard Professor Perry Miller affirmed that "Finney led America out of the eighteenth century." As a theologian, he is best known for his *Revival Lectures* and his *Systematic Theology*.

LOUIS GIFFORD PARKHURST, JR., is pastor of Christ Community Church in Oklahoma City, Oklahoma. He garnered a B.A. and an M.A. from the University of Oklahoma and an M.Div. degree from Princeton Theological Seminary. He is married and the father of two children. This is his fourteenth volume of the works of Charles G. Finney for Bethany House Publishers.

CONTENTS

PREFACE

The New Testament speaks of two types of obedience to God: legal obedience and gospel obedience.

Legal obedience comes from fear and hope. Under legal obedience, a person who professes to be a Christian obeys the law of God out of fear that if he does not, he will go to hell, and from the hope that if he does, he will go to heaven. He is living the experience of Romans, chapter seven, so ably discussed by Finney in *Principles of Victory* and *Principles of Liberty*.

Contrarily, gospel obedience flows from love for God and our fellowman. Gospel obedience is a state of benevolence, from whence flows benevolent action. It is not an obedience that seeks a selfish end—such as salvation and eternal bliss. Rather, it loves and obeys God because of who God is and for His own sake, and does so especially out of gratitude for personal salvation made possible through Jesus Christ and His atoning death. Gospel obedience flows from faith, and is a work of faith. It cannot be separated from saving faith in Jesus Christ, and it is always faith working by love.

Principles of Christian Obedience is a series of lectures that will help us distinguish between legal and gospel obe-

dience, and the principles will help us to live out gospel obedience in practical, everyday ways.

In our day and age, we need the timeless message of these
lectures. Too often, many who profess to be Christians do not
live according to biblical morality and the absolute stan-
dards of behavior God has clearly revealed. Too many mis-
takenly believe that by one simple affirmation of faith or
acceptance of some intellectual truth, or by repeating one
"sinner's prayer" respecting Jesus Christ and His atoning
death, they are thereby saved and will go to heaven when
they die. This mistaken notion of saving faith is nullified in
these lectures.

Today, the problems we face are not only because of legal
obedience to God's law versus gospel obedience, but for lack
of *any* obedience to His laws! For many, the gospel of Jesus
Christ has become a license to sin, a certificate that guar-
antees heaven to those who on earth practice unholy living.
Yet, Finney avoids the legalism that many Christians become in bondage to in their effort to live holy lives. The
careful balance and definition of Christian truths that Finney lived and preached will transform people's thinking today, and bring them into gospel liberty and victorious living,
if they will study, pray through, and practice the teaching.

In sequence of publication, *Principles of Christian Obedience* follows *Principles of Faith* and *Principles of Salvation*.
This is the correct sequence. However, I should mention that
this book was promised earlier, when on page 11 of *Principles
of Sanctification* I relayed to the reader a different order of
publication. With respect to that plan, I will say that I intended to publish Finney's practical applications for lay people in *Principles of Christian Obedience*, but discovered that
these applications followed the more theological treatment
of sanctification found in the book *Principles of Sanctification*.

The original dates of publication for Finney's lectures,
should you wish to study them in order, are included in the
"Principles Series." Suffice to say here that Timothy Smith

edited *The Promise of the Spirit*, lectures from *The Oberlin Evangelist*, 1839. *Principles of Sanctification* includes the first nine lectures from *The Oberlin Evangelist* published in 1840, and *Principles of Christian Obedience* includes the rest of Finney's sermons from 1840. The forthcoming *Principles of Consecration* will include Finney's lectures and sermons from 1841–42. And *Principles of Holiness* includes his sermons from 1843, plus a few others. His best devotional book on sanctification is *Principles of Union With Christ*, which is from lectures published in 1847. His letters on sanctification can be found in *Principles of Discipleship*.

I wish to thank my wife Patricia for typing the lectures and sermons in this book. As pastor of a new church in Oklahoma City, I could never have completed this book had she not typed these sermons for me and supported my work in many other ways.

I would also like to thank Jack Key, librarian of The Mayo Clinic, in Rochester, Minnesota, for allowing me to use his facilities and equipment as I studied the microfilms of *The Oberlin Evangelist*.

I have done the compiling and editing for publication, and the editors at Bethany House Publishers make other revisions as they see fit, and do a beautiful job of printing this series.

As the books have progressed, you may have noticed that the style of editing has changed somewhat to suit the needs of modern readers. In the first books, the sermons and lectures were almost identical to the originals. In subsequent books, I have condensed long wordy sentences, and have eliminated the numbering system used in the originals. Having published several of Finney's sermons and lectures, I feel confident that I have not distorted his thought through my editing. Furthermore, I have not "edited out" anything I might disagree with or would have preferred Finney had said differently. Since I agree with Finney, insofar as I understand him, probably ninety-eight percent of the time, I have had no problem with anything published in this series.

I believe that a consistent victorious Christian life of service can be built upon Finney's principles, because they are true to the Bible and God's moral government. These are principles we can use as we "Build Christ's Church."

With love in the Risen Lamb,
L. G. Parkhurst, Jr.

1

UNBELIEF

"So we see that they could not enter in because of unbelief" (Hebrews 3:19).
"He that believeth not, shall be damned" (Mark 16:16).

In discussing this subject I will show what unbelief is, some of its developments and manifestations, how unreasonable it is, and its causes or occasions and wickedness.

What unbelief is

Unbelief is the absence or the opposite of faith.

Faith is a *felt, conscious, practical* confidence in the character, providence and Word of God. Faith is a *conscious assurance* that what God has said shall come to pass. Faith is such an *inward* and *felt assurance* and hearty and joyful embracing of the truth that a corresponding feeling and action is produced which excludes doubt. Therefore, unbelief is a real withholding of this inward, felt, conscious assurance or confidence. Unbelief is a state of mind that leaves the conduct uninfluenced by the truths of God; such a withholding of confidence as to leave both body and soul under the influence of error; to pursue a course as if the truths of God were not true.

15

Some of the developments and manifestations of unbelief

One manifestation of unbelief is ignorance of religious truths. Unbelief is the only principle that influences a moral being to be uninformed on religious issues. The infinitely great and weighty truths of the faith make an impression as a matter of course upon a moral being in proportion to the fullness with which they are apprehended and believed.

One development of unbelief is worldly mindedness. Only the principle of unbelief would motivate a human being to give himself up to the pursuit of worldly goods. Let him but possess that inward, felt assurance that the infinitely great truths of Christianity are realities, and the world will at once dwindle to insignificance in his estimation. It will appear to be a very small thing whether he does or does not possess the wealth, the honors, the friendship, or wisdom of this world. And to spend his time and give up his thoughts to accumulating anything that this world can give or take away is entirely unnatural to a mind that believes in eternal realities.

Another development of unbelief is a spirit of worry or corroding and peace-destroying anxiety upon any subject. Can a person who has the conscious and felt assurance that the infinitely faithful God is committed to the supply of all his temporal, spiritual and eternal needs experience the worry and anxiety of one who has no such belief?

Worldly conversation is another development of unbelief. Can the infinitely interesting things of Christianity be felt conscious realities to the mind whose conversation is worldly? Impossible! "Out of the abundance of the heart the mouth speaketh." For a person to converse upon that which does not occupy his thoughts is impossible. And if eternal things are felt realities, realities in which the heart takes the deepest and most joyful interest, it is impossible that the conversation should not correspond with this state of mind.

Insensibility to the state of the Church and the world is

another manifestation of unbelief. A person can no more avoid being excited by the spiritual state of the Church and the world if Christian truth is a reality to his mind, than he could avoid excitement if the house or town in which he lived was all in flames.

Insensibility to the abuse which is everywhere heaped upon God is a manifestation of unbelief. If the existence, character and omnipresence of God, with their kindred truths, be realities, it would give the one who realized this unutterable pain to witness the abuse which is heaped upon God by His creatures. Could you see your father, mother, wife, husband, teacher, or dearest earthly friend, abused, and experience no agony? Impossible!

Apathy in regard to spreading the gospel proves that you do not believe it. What abhorrence there was in this country about the famine in the Cape Verde Islands, and the subject of the oppression of the Greeks. What public interest was awakened, and what pains were taken to send them relief. Should a famine pervade Europe or America, what a universal sympathy would be awakened, and how the concerned population would motivate themselves with thousands of tons of provisions to supply their needs. This is natural, reasonable, right and according to the laws of our being. But how shall we account for the apathy of the Church in reference to starving souls going to hell without the gospel? Because of the very apt principle that almost nobody believes it! It is impossible to account for it upon any other supposition.

Neglect of the Bible is another development of unbelief. What is the Bible? What are its claims? What does it profess to reveal to mankind? It claims to be a revelation from God to men, a history of their past lives, and a revelation of their future destiny. From every point of view, it is without doubt the most fascinating book that ever existed. And yet, almost all people, even in Christian lands, are in a great measure unacquainted with its truths and manifestly care but little about them. Now, it seems impossible that the reason for this lack of knowledge is owing to any other principle than that of unbelief. If people believed the Bible, they would search after its meaning as they would for hidden treasures. They would not, could not, rest satisfied until they possessed every practical truth contained in it.

Unbelief often manifests itself in the interpretation of the Bible. Unitarians can see no sufficient evidence of the divinity of Jesus Christ. Why? Because of unbelief. It is remarkable to see to what an extent unbelief is the basis of biblical interpretation in the Church! Examine, for example, 2 Corinthians 6:16–18: "And what agreement hath the temple of God with idols? for ye are the temple of the living God; as God hath said, I will dwell in them, and walk in them; and I will be their God, and they shall be my people. Wherefore come out from among them, and be ye separate, saith the Lord, and touch not the unclean thing; and I will receive you, and will be a Father unto you, and ye shall be my sons and daughters, saith the Lord Almighty." Now what an infinitely different inference the Apostle drew from these promises from what is generally drawn. See 2 Corinthians 7:1: "Having therefore these promises, dearly beloved, let us cleanse ourselves from all filthiness of the flesh and spirit, perfecting holiness in the fear of God." Here Paul saw in these promises such a fullness of meaning as to infer at once from them, even if there should be no other kindred promises in the Bible, the practicality of attaining a state of entire sanctification or holiness in this life. Mark the strength of his language. He exhorts them to cleanse themselves from all filthiness of the flesh and spirit, and to perfect holiness in the fear of God.

How easy it is to see that his faith apprehended an infinitely greater fullness in the meaning of these promises than is seen by the heart of unbelief. And why should he not make the inference he does? He says: "Ye are the temple of the living God; as God hath said, I will dwell in them, and walk in them; and I will be their God, and they shall be my people. Wherefore come out from among them, and be ye separate, saith the Lord, and touch not the unclean thing; and I will receive you, and will be a Father unto you, and ye shall be my sons and daughters, saith the Lord Almighty." Certainly the inference which the Apostle draws in the first verse of the next chapter, the exhortation or command as it may be regarded to avail ourselves of the provisions, and perfect holiness in the fear of God, is eminently reasonable. And yet unbelief sees no satisfactory reason, either in these or in all the promises of the Bible, to warrant the conclusion that as a matter of fact any such state is attainable in this life.

Listen, for example, to a spiritually minded woman converse with her minister about the great fullness there is in Christ. While she speaks in general terms he consents to all she says, that there is indeed unspeakable and infinite fullness in Christ. But where does she see this fullness? In the scripture declarations and promises of God's Word. Now let her begin to quote them one after another as she understands them, and he will probably take exception to her views of every one of them, and consider her notions as utterly extravagant, and perhaps fanatical. He consents in general to the fullness that is in Christ, but explains away in detail all the evidence of that fullness as apprehended by a spiritual mind. The truth is, a spiritual mind, and a spiritual mind only, understands the real meaning of the Bible. And nothing is more common than for people in a state of unbelief to read again and again any and every passage in the Bible without grasping the real meaning of the Holy Spirit. A person in this state of mind has, as a matter of fact, never begun to understand the fullness there is in Jesus Christ, nor the depth and extent of meaning in the declarations and promises of the Scriptures.

Stumbling at difficulties is another manifestation of unbelief. A large class of minds seems not to be under the influence of evidence, especially upon those subjects that in any way clash with their own interests. However weighty the evidence may be, the suggestion of the least difficulty is to them an insurmountable stumbling block, and the shadow of an objection seems to bring them to a standstill in regard to all progress in reform, giving them right over to the dominion of appetite, lust and every form of selfishness. They are eagle-eyed in discovering a contradiction, and seem not to have the faculty at all to answer and resolve the conflict. Any question or difficulty is sufficient reason for their resisting even the evidence of miracles. Logical proof itself does not in such cases seem to move their hearts. If an answer to their difficulty is suggested to them, they take no heed to it, for it is evident in their subsequent behavior, and the next day you will find them still hanging on to their doubts regarding uncomprehended portions, for they go on stubbornly in their sins. This is a most guilty and abominable state of mind.

With what loathing did this same attitude manifest itself among the Jews, when neither the life, the doctrine, the miracles, the death, nor the resurrection of Christ could convince them. Certain preconceived notions of what Christ would be, and certain false and absurd interpretations of prophecy in regard to Him were sufficient objections in their minds to break the power of all the evidence with which Christ brought forth the demonstration of His Messiahship.

It is both amazing and distressing to see how unbelief will paralyze the power of testimony in favor of truth, insomuch that no weight or accumulation of evidence can gain ascendancy over the intellect and the heart in the presence of even the most ridiculous objections.

Now contrast the state of mind of unbelief with the conduct of Abraham, the "father of the faithful." God had promised to make him "a father of many nations." But the fulfillment was delayed until both he and his wife were at such an age that but for the promise of God it was utterly unreasonable to expect that Sarah would have an heir. Study Romans 4:19–21: "And being not weak in faith, he considered not his own body now dead, when he was about a hundred years old, neither yet the deadness of Sarah's womb. He staggered not at the promise of God through unbelief; but was strong in faith, giving glory to God; and being fully persuaded, that what He had promised, He was able also to perform." The fact that he and Sarah were nearly a hundred years old was not a sufficient objection to set aside the testimony of God in his mind. And he remained firm in the opinion that His promise would be performed.

Witness his conduct also in offering up Isaac as a burnt sacrifice. Here is another beautiful illustration of the power of faith as contrasted with unbelief. After a long time, his beloved Isaac was born, who also was to be the father of many nations, and through whom the promised Messiah was to come. Before Isaac could become the father of any offspring, God commanded Abraham to offer him as a burnt sacrifice. So unshaken was Abraham's confidence that he appears not to have felt the least uneasiness about the event.

Feeling probably that it might stagger Sarah's faith, he apparently did not communicate it to her, but rose up calmly on the morning after the command was given and proceeded to the spot with the wood and necessary implements. Obviously, he expected to actually offer him according to the command of God. And in fact, as far as the mental act was concerned, he really did offer him. The Bible says: "By faith Abraham, when he was tried, offered up Isaac: and he that had received the promises offered up his only begotten son, of whom it was said, That in Isaac shall thy seed by called: accounting that God was able to raise him up, even from the dead; from whence also he received him in a figure."

Observe also the conduct of Abraham in regard to the promised land. God had promised to give him that land, and to his "seed for a thousand generations." Now Abraham lived in this country as a stranger: "By faith he sojourned in the land of promise, as in a strange country, dwelling in tabernacles with Isaac and Jacob, the heirs with him of the same promise." When his beloved Sarah died, he bought the cave of Machpelah for a burial place, and in this cave he was afterwards buried himself. His seed did not inherit the land for more than four hundred years, which shows that Abraham understood the promise would be fulfilled to his descendants, and remained "strong in faith, giving glory to God." How vastly different was the state of Abraham's mind from that to which I have alluded before, where a trifling contradiction can stumble a mind, and paralyze or overthrow all confidence in the testimony of God.

Confiding more in men than in God is another development of unbelief. How common it is for even professed Christians to have more confidence in the prayers of some mere man than in the intercession of Christ; and to place more reliance upon the word of man than upon the Word of God, and as a matter of course, to be more influenced by the opinions, or the mere say-so of men, than by the testimony and even the oath of God. If you were to ask them if they had more confidence in man than in God, they would say no. But, as a matter of fact, they have, whether they are aware of it or not. Their conduct proves that their faith is not in God, but in man. As an illustration of this, witness the anxieties and worries of multitudes of God's professed children on the subject of temporal provision for their families. If some wealthy man would give them a bond or mortgage, a bank check, or even a promissory note for ten or twenty thousand dollars, they would feel perfectly at rest in regard to the supply of their temporal wants. Their faith or confidence in this security would have its practical influence. It would allay all their fears, silence all their worries and anxieties, and they would feel it reasonable to be at rest upon that subject. Why then does the promise, the oath and security of God not forever hush and silence all worry in the hearts of God's professed people? "Trust in the Lord and do good, and thou shalt dwell in the land, and verily thou shalt be fed."

Surely this and multitudes of kindred promises are infinitely higher and better security than can be given by the wealthiest men on earth. The Bible contains the bond and mortgage, promissory note and oath of Jehovah, who cannot lie, and who has the resources of the Universe at His command.

Now let me ask you, what state of mind is it which does not repose practically and with as much confidence in these promises, as in human commitments and securities? What do you mean by your doubt? Why do you not rest? What higher possible security can you have? What shocking unbelief, and how infinitely provoking to God, that the promise of mortal man is so much more confided in than the promise and oath of God!

Murmuring at the providence of God is another of the developments of unbelief. Some people are almost always in anxiety as to whether things will go right under the providence of God. They are full of fearfulness and trembling, and even terror, lest the winds, the weather, the seasons, and a thousand other things should not be exactly agreeable to their wish. They are continually murmuring at what is daily coming to pass; manifesting in a most certain manner, either that they are entirely opposed to God, or that they are infidels and have no belief in His providence. They manifest an utter lack of confidence in His existence, wisdom and providence; and would fain have almost everything in the government of the material universe different from what it is. Today, you are sorry that it rains. Tonight, you fear there will be frost. Tomorrow, you fear there will be a high wind. In the summer, that there will be drought; and in the winter, that there will be too much or too little snow. Indeed, the unbelief of many people keeps them in a state of almost perpetual and God-dishonoring anxiety. And is it not astonishing that this state of mind is so seldom regarded as being the very essence of all that is criminal and abominable in the sight of God?

The absence of a joyful acquiescence in the whole will of God as expressed either in His works, providence or Word is also a result of unbelief. If a person has entire confidence in God in all things, he will have a supreme complacency in the will of God. He will not merely submit without rebellion, but will be joyfully acquiescent in all the works, ways and will of God. Whatever the weather is; whatever the seasons are;

whatever God does or permits to be done, is, so far as God is concerned, most sweetly acquiesced in by a soul exercising faith.

Maintaining a false hope is another manifestation of unbelief. God has said, "If any man hath this hope in him (i.e., the true Christian hope), he purifieth himself even as Christ is pure." Now, how many thousands of professing Christians are there whose hope does not even in a small way manifest itself in a holy life? They are just as certain of it as they are of their own existence, and they hold on to it tenaciously, determined to stake their eternal destiny upon it. But what is this but virtually basing their eternal salvation upon the notion that the complete declaration of God is *not* true. They are hoping in hope for hope's sake alone, but not believing God for all that stems from a true hope in all that His word implies. It is not only questioning this and multitudes of kindred passages, it is not merely denying them, it is not merely making God a liar, but it is virtually saying, "I stake my eternal salvation on the fact that these declarations of God are not true." Upon what other conceivable or possible ground can they hold fast to their false hope? They seem to be entirely ignorant that their hope is the result of sheer infidelity. They have not so much as a conviction that the Bible is true. If they had, their hope would perish like the moth in a moment. How many thousands of cases are there in which professing Christians, as soon as they become convicted, and have a realizing sense of the truth of the Bible, yield up their false hopes, all the while never seeming to know that the very fact they ever had a hope was attributable entirely to their unbelief.

A conscious refusal to enter into the rest of faith is another product of unbelief. God has said, "Thou wilt keep him in perfect peace whose mind is stayed on thee, because he *trusteth* in thee." What multitudes there are, who are continually disquieting themselves, not only about their temporal but about their spiritual state, simply because they refuse to believe that in Christ they are complete; that in

Him all fullness dwells; that in Him every demand of their nature, everything that they can need for time and eternity, is made secure by the promise and oath of God. A state of unbelief is very like a mind in the midst of some agonizing dream:

> Where the wreck'd desponding thought,
> From wave to wave of fancied misery,
> At random drives, her helm of reason lost.

How often a man in some distressing dream imagines himself poor—perhaps he and his family are destitute and in want of all things, perhaps in debt, and in prison, with no means of payment, surrounded with the darkest and most forbidding prospects on every side, and on every subject; no friends, no home, no employment, no confidence in himself or in anybody else. The consummation of wretchedness and despair has overwhelmed him until some sudden noise or disturbance awakens him, and behold, he is at home, in bed, in health, and the reverse of all his crazy dream is true. "I thank God," he exclaims, "that all this is but a dream. I thought I had no home, no friends, no health; was in debt, persecuted, imprisoned; saw no help, for time or eternity, but all this was a dream. I am now awake, and blessed be God the reality is all the reverse of my vain imaginings." Just so, faith breaks up the spell that binds the mind in all its doubts, perplexities and anxieties, and introduces it into a state of perfect rest in Christ. Just as the wretched unbeliever who felt condemned owed ten thousand talents to divine justice and had nothing with which to pay, he struggled, agonized, prayed, read, searched, looked every way, and saw neither help nor hope.

Remembering the past filled his soul with shame, and was agonizing beyond expression. Present circumstances are discouraging and fill his mind with forebodings of future wrath. The future is as dark as midnight; there seems to be "no eye to pity, and no arm can save." It would seem as if the aggregate of all conceivable woes, temporal, spiritual and eternal, were in reserve for him. But, ah! He apprehends faith in Christ, and how instantaneously the whole scene is changed. "Can it be possible?" he exclaims. "Oh what a wretched, horrible pit of miry clay is that from which my feet are taken. This is indeed everlasting rock. My goings are indeed established. I see an ample provision, not only for the forgiveness of all my past sins, but for all my present, future, utmost, conceivable or possible wants. The provision is absolutely boundless, and made sure by the promise of Him who cannot lie. 'Return unto thy rest, O my soul, for the Lord hath dealt bountifully with thee.' Is it true that I have such a Savior, in whom all fullness dwells? Am I complete in Him? Is He my wisdom, my righteousness, my sanctification, and my redemption? It is surely so. It is as certain as my existence. Oh, I feel as if my soul were in an ocean of sweet and boundless rest and peace, and my God hath said, 'Thou wilt keep him in perfect peace whose mind is stayed on Thee.' " Now, any refusal or neglect to enter at once into this state of mind is unbelief. And, dearly beloved, if this is so, let me inquire, was not that a most pertinent question of Christ, "When I come, shall I find faith on the earth?"

Another repercussion of unbelief is a lack of an inward assurance and felt confidence that God's promises will be fulfilled. Take for instance, James 1:5–7: "If any of you lack wisdom, let him ask of God, that giveth to all men liberally, and upbraideth not; and it shall be given him. But let him ask in faith, nothing wavering: for he that wavereth is like a wave of the sea driven with the wind and tossed. For let not that man think that he shall receive any thing of the Lord." Now who will pretend to question this truth? And yet, who believes it? Who has the inward assurance that is essential to faith, that he shall be taught of God? Who comes to Him with the same assurance that he will be taught, as a student goes to his professor with some question with which he knows him to be familiar? The student goes to his teacher with confidence and expectation, with as much faith as he has in his own existence, that he will be given an answer.

He does not go in a negative state of mind, because he knows that his teacher is knowledgeable of the subject of his inquiry and that he will surely lead him to an understanding of it. Now, why does he expect this? Because this is the business of his teacher, and because he has pledged himself to instruct his pupils. So has God pledged himself, in the strongest and most solemn manner. Do we not then have a right; are we not bound to come to God for instruction with as much felt assurance as we would exercise in going to a human teacher? Consider also 1 Thessalonians 5:23, 24: "And the very God of peace sanctify you wholly; and I pray God your whole spirit and soul and body be preserved blameless unto the coming of our Lord Jesus Christ. Faithful is he that calleth you, who also will do it." Now here the Apostle prays for the entire sanctification of spirit, soul, and body, and that our whole being may be preserved blameless unto the coming of our Lord Jesus Christ; and then pledges the faithfulness of God: "Faithful is He that calleth you, who also will do it." Now do we not have a right; are we not bound to exercise the utmost confidence, and to have a felt and strong assurance of mind that what is promised here shall come to pass? And whatever is short of this is unbelief.

See also the case of Paul, in 2 Corinthians 12:9: "And He said unto me, My grace is sufficient for thee: for my strength is made perfect in weakness. Most gladly therefore will I rather glory in my infirmities, that the power of Christ may rest upon me." God had given him "a thorn in the flesh, a messenger of Satan to buffet him, lest he should be exalted above measure." But Paul, fearing that it would injure his influence, besought the Lord thrice that it might depart from him. But Christ replied, "My grace is sufficient for thee: for my grace is made perfect in weakness." Now this entirely satisfied the mind of Paul, and he immediately adds, "Most gladly therefore will I rather glory in my infirmities, that the power of Christ may rest upon me." It appears that he, at once, felt an inward, conscious assurance that allayed all his fears in regard to the influence of this thorn in the flesh, and enabled him to say, "Therefore, I take pleasure in infirmities." Now I suppose this to be as true of every man as of Paul: Christ's grace is sufficient for him, in any circumstances in which the providence of God can place him; and that nothing but unbelief prevents any Christian from experiencing the utmost confidence and the inward unwavering assurance of mind that Christ's grace is sufficient for him.

Even asking God for an inward assurance of what He has promised is another sign of unbelief. Suppose you had promised your little son something that he knew you were abundantly able to give, but your promise did not satisfy him. He is uneasy and continues to ask whether you will certainly do it. And notwithstanding your most solemn assurances, he should come to you and say, "Father, I want you to do something that will give me an inward assurance that you will fulfill your promise. I feel very uncertain about it. I can't picture in my mind that you will actually do it. I want to feel sure in my heart that I shall have it. I want that inward assurance without which I cannot rest." Now would you not consider this a downright insult to you? Suppose you had not only repeatedly given him your word, but had confirmed it by an oath; and yet he had no felt confidence in your veracity. Asking for additional assurances would be regarded by you with grief and indignation. You would consider it a virtual charging you with falsehood and perjury; and you would consider it a humiliation to listen to such a request and furnish further assurances, even if it were in your power.

Now let me ask, is it considered by Christians that all asking for an inward felt assurance for that strong confidence that quiets the mind is but an instance of shocking unbelief? Why do you not *feel* that assurance already? Cannot the promise and oath of God convince, persuade and assure you that what He has said shall come to pass? You ought to know that the absence of this felt assurance is a virtual charging Him with falsehood and perjury. All pleading the promises of God without this inward, felt, unwavering assurance of mind, where the promise is plain and the application just, is an instance of unbelief.

When Paul prayed against the thorn in the flesh, he had no express promise that that thorn should be removed. He was not therefore bound to believe that it would be. So Christ had no express promise that His agony in the garden should be removed. In neither of these cases did perfect faith in God imply the belief that the particular things requested would be granted. But had there been an express promise in either or both of these cases, they both would have had the right, and been under an obligation to exercise the most unwavering assurance, that the specific blessing promised should be granted. It should be understood, therefore, that in pleading the promises of God with a just apprehension and understanding of them, every state of mind is unbelief that falls short of the most unwavering assurance that the thing promised shall be granted according to the true tenor and meaning of the promise. All uneasiness of mind in regard to the event—all unhappiness through fear, that it will not be granted—everything short of the utmost repose of mind in the veracity of God, is God-dishonoring unbelief.

Suppose a student received letters from his father containing the strongest assurances that he would supply all his needs, giving him the fullest liberty to draw on him at any time for any amount he needed. Suppose it were well known that his father's fortune was very ample, and there could be no doubt of his ability to fulfill his promises. Further suppose that his father's promises were backed up by oaths and the most abundant assurances that could be expressed in words. Now suppose this student is seen to be full of anxiety and worry about his support; laying his plans and making arrangements to help himself entirely independent of his father's aid. It would be evident at once that he had no confidence in his father's word. Everybody would infer at once that however rich his father might be, no confidence could be placed in his veracity. Everyone might say, "You see how it is. This young man is acquainted with his father. We have seen his letters. We know what abundant promises he has given, and yet it is a fact his son has not a particle of confidence in these declarations." The inference of a lack of integrity in his father would be natural and certain.

Now, Christian, did you ever consider how horrible your conduct is in the eyes of an unbelieving world? They know what promises your Father has made, and they see by your anxiety and worldly-mindedness how little confidence you have in these promises. They witness your foreboding and worldly spirit, and think in their hearts, these Christians know that God is not to be trusted, for as a matter of fact they have no confidence in His promises. How can you in any way more deeply wound the Christian faith than by this unbelief, and worse still, more fully and certainly dishonor God? It is a most shameful declaration in the most impressive manner possible that you believe God to be a liar!

Not realizing that Christ died for you in particular is another ramification of unbelief. The Apostle says that "Christ tasted death for every man." Now what state of mind is that which does not realize and feel assured that He died for you? There is a great deal of complaining in the Church that individuals cannot feel as if Christ died for them in particular. If He died for *every* man, He died for you as an individual, and any lack of realizing and feeling the inward assurance of this is unbelief. It is the mind's hiding itself in the darkness of its own selfishness. You believe that He died for *all* men, that He tasted death for *every* man; but cannot be convinced He died for you. Thus you parry obligation and deny the realization that your sins nailed Him to the cross, and that your soul is guilty of His death; that His love has rolled a weight of responsibility upon you. It is time for you to realize that this is nothing but unbelief, and a virtual contradiction of the truth that "Christ tasted death for every man." No wonder your heart is not subdued. No wonder you are in bondage to your sins. No wonder your lusts and appetites have dominion over you, while you are so unbelieving as not to realize that what God has said is true. All lack of appropriating the truth, promises and warnings of God to yourself is unbelief. There is a remarkable disposition in most who profess to be Christians to mingle with the crowd, to confuse their own sins, wants, and all that concerns themselves individually with the sins and wants of the Church at large. But truth does no good in the world unless it has its individual application. It sanctifies only when it is appropriated, taken home, and applied to the individual conscience and heart.

Not to appropriate truth to yourself is like an individual who is invited to a feast along with many others. But he does not go himself because the invitation is general. Or when he is there, does not himself partake of the food, because the provision was made for all the guests. The grand reason why he should go as an individual, why he should partake personally without hesitation, is because the provision is general but personal, and everyone has equal right and is expected to partake of what is provided for the enjoyment of all.

How shocking it is that so many professing Christians let the provisions of the gospel lie before them, and all the promises of the Bible cluster around them, and yet because the provisions are so ample, and the promise is to everyone who will partake, stand and look on in their unbelief and starve to death!

(This material is continued in the next sermon.)

2

UNBELIEF/PART 2

"So we see that they could not enter in because of unbelief" (Hebrews 3:19).
"He that believeth not, shall be damned" (Mark 16:16b).

To continue my last sermon, I will begin by discussing the unreasonableness of unbelief.

Unbelief is unreasonable because confidence in testimony is natural to people. This is a law of our being. And until selfishness comes to take possession of our hearts and blind us in respect to any truth or thing that opposes our wills or inclinations, it is one of the easiest and most natural exercises of the human mind to confide in testimony. This is strikingly evident in the conduct of very young children. Unbelief is unreasonable because confidence in testimony is a natural exercise of the mind through every period of life.

Society could not exist without it. All the business transactions of the world revolve around this law of the mind: confidence in testimony. Everyone would agree that no such thing as government, order or happiness could exist in any community without confidence.

Unbelief is unreasonable because all evidence is in favor of unlimited and heart-felt confidence in the character and Word of God. Creation and Providence confirm the truths of the Bible, and, when properly understood, give forth the same lessons as far as they go. The heavens above, the earth beneath, everything within and without us, goes to confirm the proposition that it is the perfection of reason to place the most unlimited confidence in God. The works of creation and providence, when duly studied and understood, exhibit God in such a light as not only to confirm the testimony of the Bible, but to lead to the conclusion that the Bible means as much as it appears to mean; that God is to be trusted for all that He has promised, and that His promises mean what they say.

Unbelief is entirely unreasonable, because the atonement is the highest possible demonstration of God's intention to do to every human being all the good He *wisely* can. Certainly it is the opposite of everything that is reasonable to suppose that God should give His only begotten Son to die for all peoples, and then willingly withhold any lesser good which He can *wisely* bestow upon them. And this is the reasoning and the conclusion of the Apostle: "He that spared not His own Son, but delivered Him up for us all, how shall He not with Him freely give us all things?"

In the Atonement alone we have the highest evidence that can be given of the infinitely great love of God to every one of us—a degree of evidence that demands the most heartfelt confidence in His character, government, word, promises, providence, and carefulness for our temporal and eternal good. Reader, did you ever consider the amount and force of evidence contained in the Atonement, that God really loves you, that He loves you so much as to give His only begotten and well-beloved Son to die in your place? What higher evidence could you ask, expect or conceive, that any other being loved you, than for that one to give his own Son to die to preserve your life. And should such a thing take place, would you not consider it the most shocking, unnatural and abominable conduct conceivable to withhold confidence in that one's love for you?

The Atonement so illustrates and confirms the love of God

to us as to render it in the highest degree reasonable to put the most liberal construction on all His promises of good to us. Let me refer again to 2 Corinthians 6:16–18, and 7:1: "And what agreement hath the temple of God with idols? for ye are the temple of the living God; as God hath said, I will dwell in them, and walk in them; and I will be their God, and they shall be my people. Wherefore come out from among them, and be ye separate, saith the Lord, and touch not the unclean thing; and I will receive you, and will be a Father unto you, and ye shall be my sons and daughters, saith the Lord Almighty." "Having therefore these promises, dearly beloved, let us cleanse ourselves from all filthiness of the flesh and spirit, perfecting holiness in the fear of God." I have already said that from these promises, "I will dwell in them and walk in them, and I will be their God and they shall be my people; I will receive you and be a Father unto you, and ye shall be my sons and daughters," the Apostle infers the practicality of entirely cleansing ourselves from all filthiness of the flesh and spirit, and of perfecting holiness in the fear of God.

Now I ask you, is this not one of the most reasonable inferences in the world? In the light of the Atonement, and considering the infinitely great love of God, as therein manifested, how much is it reasonable to expect God to mean in such promises as these? What is naturally and fully implied in these kindred promises, in view of His infinite love and the bountifulness of His heart as expressed in the Atonement? I do not hesitate to say that it is in the highest degree unreasonable, in view of these promises alone, to draw any other inference than that which the Apostle drew from them. And what shall we say of the almost numberless exceeding great and precious promises that were given for the express purpose of making us partakers of the divine nature? It must be admitted that they bring us at once to the conclusion that it is utterly unreasonable to believe anything less than that God will "sanctify us, spirit, soul, and body, and preserve us blameless unto the coming of our Lord Jesus Christ."

The evidence contained in the Atonement of the infinitely great love of God to us is, if such a thing be possible, confirmed and strengthened by the great patience and forbearance of God exercised toward this world since the Atonement—His patience and perseverance in using means to induce mankind to accept the Atonement—His striving by His Spirit, and all the influences He exerts to sanctify and save seem to pile demonstration upon demonstration of His infinite love and disposition to do us good. Now certainly nothing on earth or in hell can be conceived of as more unreasonable than unbelief.

To stumble at any difficulty which may lie in the way is utterly unreasonable, for these difficulties are just what we ought to expect, and a moment's consideration would show us that it is naturally impossible it should not be so. We are but in the infancy of our being. Only a very little could be, to our finite minds, explained to us in this world. There is scarcely a thing in the universe that does not involve, in minds like ours, mysteries, which we do not and cannot understand. Our own nature, the nature and constitution of everything around us, presents to us mysteries as impenetrable, and difficulties as great, so far as we know, as any of the truths of Christianity. And yet, on other than Christian issues, we receive testimony, and believe facts, where we cannot comprehend all the philosophy and explanation of them. We are shut up to this necessity in relation to almost everything in the universe. And so it follows how infinitely unreasonable it is, in the midst of our ignorance of material things, to stumble at difficulties, perplex ourselves with mysteries, and withhold confidence in the testimony of God simply because the *why* and the *how* are not in many instances understood by us.

It is vastly unreasonable not to feel an *inward assurance* that God's promises shall all be fulfilled. If I owed you a thousand dollars, you might have reason to feel insecure in regard to the payment, and should you come to me and say, "I doubt your ability to pay. I need to feel at rest about this debt, and wish you to give me further security," this might be very reasonable. But will you ask further security of God? Who will underwrite for Him? Who or what can make His promises more secure? Would you have a warranty deed of the universe, a bond and mortgage, signed, sealed and delivered, and registered in the court of heaven?

Of course, all this you have and more too. For "God, willing more abundantly to show unto the heirs of promise the immutability of His counsel, confirmed it by an oath: that by two immutable things, in which it was impossible for God to lie, we might have a strong consolation, who have fled for refuge to lay hold upon the hope set before us." And yet you may say, "But, I want to feel in my heart the assurance that God will fulfill His promises to me". *Feel* in your heart? Do not the promise and oath of God make you feel in your heart that what He has said shall come to pass? What an infinitely unreasonable and abominable state of mind is this that can complain of the lack of a felt assurance that the God of infinite truth will not lie? What more security can He give? Who can post His bail? Who or what in the universe can make His promise more certain?

Now suppose that you had the bond and mortgage, and the oath of the richest man in America for a million dollars. Would not your neighbors consider you a mad man if you did not feel in your heart that your debt was secure? Yes, you would be pronounced deranged by every court of law or equity in the land. I recall to mind a case where a man of wealth became a hypochondriac and made himself continually unhappy lest he and his family should become paupers. His wealthy connections, to relieve his mind, offered to secure to him a large amount of money annually for the support of his family. He replied, "That would be of no avail, for 'riches would take to themselves wings,' and he could put no confidence in any such security." Finally, a commission of mental incapacity was issued to secure his property, and he was pronounced mentally deranged in view of these developments of mind.

Now I do not hesitate to say that his state of mind was almost the perfection of reason, when compared with the infinite unreasonableness and insanity of not feeling the utmost assurance that all the promises of God should be fulfilled. What was there so very unreasonable in the conduct of this man? That he refused to trust in human security and responsibility for the maintenance of his family. Now in one sense this might have been unreasonable, and the court may have done right in pronouncing him mentally incapacitated. But if this is insanity, what state of mind is that which cannot confide in the testimony and oath of the infinite and ever blessed God of truth? Why, beloved, if God has promised to maintain your family, if He has told you, "Trust in the Lord and do good, so shalt thou dwell in the land, and verily thou shalt be fed"; if the infinitely faithful God has promised to circumcise your heart and the heart of your seed, to love the Lord your God with all your heart, and all your soul; if He has promised to "sanctify you wholly, spirit, soul, and body, and preserve you blameless," is it not the widest departure from reason that can be conceived of for you not to feel assured in your heart that all this shall be done?

Causes or occasions of unbelief.

Selfishness prevents attention to the evidence of God's character. People are so taken up with seeking their own private interests as to have very little time for consideration in regard to the real character of God as manifested in the works of creation, providence and grace. People in their delirious scramble after their selfish interests almost lose the idea of even the existence of God, and to all practical purposes they often quite do this.

The selfishness of people prevents their receiving the idea that God is benevolence. Being conscious of their own selfishness, and witnessing the same principle in those all around them, they come to regard all intelligent beings as selfish. It is amazing to see how difficult it is for the human mind to be possessed of a true knowledge of God. God charges mankind for thinking that He is altogether such a one as they are. Though it is most natural for us to judge others by ourselves it is also presumptuous and blasphemous with respect to God.

The consciousness of our own hypocrisy in many things, and the repeated instances of insincerity and hypocrisy in almost all those around us, naturally begets distrust or a lack of confidence in the genuineness and disinterested benevolence of most everyone. Because we constantly compare ourselves with others and not with God, the consciousness of our own unmercifulness, and evidence of the same in others, renders it difficult to conceive of the infinite mercy of God.

The fact that people seek and think they find their happiness in getting all they can blinds their minds with regard to the fact that God's character is directly the reverse of this. Benevolence is His character; doing instead of getting, giving instead of receiving, constitute His happiness. People cry continually, "Give, give," and are never satisfied with appropriating to themselves. God, on the other hand, finds His happiness in giving and in pouring out blessings from His infinite fullness upon all who can be persuaded to receive them. People are naturally unwilling to conceive of God's character as the direct opposite of their own, and this results in unbelief. Unwillingness to believe in whatever or whoever rebukes our sin is another cause of unbelief. We have too much regard for our own reputation. Read John 5:44: "How can ye believe, which receive honor one of another, and seek not the honor that cometh from God only?" Here Christ plainly teaches that a regard for our own reputation will prevent our receiving and believing the testimony of God. Prejudice is often a fruitful source of unbelief.

To pre-judge or make up your mind on any question before you know all the facts is, of course, in the highest degree calculated to bar the mind against a knowledge and belief of the truth. Pride that keeps us in favor of error will also promote unbelief.

When a person has committed himself to the defense of any error, and therefore against any truth, he is in the greatest danger of never coming to a knowledge of the truth. He will almost of a matter of course reject in unbelief any light that might correct his darkness.

Sensuality will invariably blind one in unbelief. Let anyone give himself up to the indulgence of his appetites, and his mind will become dark as midnight to all but sensible objects. He will "walk after the sight of his eyes, and the hearing of his ears"; but is never likely to believe or know anything of God as he ought to know.

Confidence in the opinion of those who are themselves unbelieving will, of course, prevent our believing the testimony of God. This is an amazing flaw, producing unbelief. There are great multitudes who confide more in men than in God, who permit their confidence in God to be entirely undermined or destroyed by the unbelieving evasions of those who profess to have faith in God, but who in fact do not. The temptations of Satan, as everyone knows, are the occasion of much unbelief. By contradicting God and shaking the confidence of our first parents in God, he has spoiled the world.

Lack of a clear idea of what faith really is, is another cause for unbelief. Many think that they already believe, because they admit the truths of the gospel and have no consciousness of positive disbelief. They overlook the fact that faith is the mind's felt and joyful assurance of the truth of God. They are aware that they have no felt and conscious assurance. They would think it a very high and rare attainment in their Christian walk to have a felt, clear, conscious assurance that God's promises would be fulfilled to them. Thus supposing that what really constitutes the faith of the gospel is out of reach for them, they take up with something short of faith, and rest in a state of mind that is not even aware of the presence of unbelief.

Gluttony, and every other form of intemperance, breeds unbelief. Lack of self-control grieves the Spirit of God. It sensualizes and degrades the mind, bringing it into the bondage of the flesh. Our selfish will, more than anything and everything else, precludes the exercise of faith. The Jews were actually able to resist the evidence of miracles. We know how difficult it is to beget confidence in a mind against the will of the individual. Indeed the thing is impossible. Confidence is an act of the will itself. It is often amazing to see how much evidence may be accumulated and presented to the mind; and yet, the heart withholds its confidence. The truth is, people do not believe God, because they will not.

The wickedness of unbelief.

Unbelief is the maximum abomination. There is no greater perversion of right reason in the whole universe of minds as unbelief. Should the son of a great prince, who possessed immeasurable wealth, be filled with care and great anxiety about his daily bread, who would not say that he was a vastly unreasonable son and in a ludicrous state of mind? Suppose further, that to quiet his anxiety his father gave him a bond and mortgage of all that he possessed, and made him secure by every possible means. If his fears should still prevail, and he should say, "I cannot realize and feel assured in my own mind that my temporal necessities shall be supplied," who would not declare this to be a most illogical state of mind?

But how would this begin to compare with the infinite unreasonableness of that state of mind which complains that it does not realize and cannot feel assured that all its needs, spiritual and temporal, shall be supplied by God? Unbelief is the most injurious sin against God that can be committed. It implies and includes: (1) A flat denial of the integrity of His character. (2) A denial of His attributes. (3) It charges Him with hypocrisy. It actually says to God, "You made high pretensions of love to me, of your ability and willingness to supply all my needs. You professed infinite compassion, and boasted of your infinite grace. You avert that you are able and willing to meet the necessities of my nature. You have given your pledge and oath, and have sworn by two immutable things by which you say it is impossible for you to lie; and yet, Lord, I do not feel in my heart that there is a word of truth in all these professions. I have no confidence in them, and am not convinced in my mind that they are true." (4) It is plainly charging God with lying, and that, too, under oath. (5) It is charging Him with infinite folly and inconsistency. Indeed unbelief cannot lodge in any mind without virtually charging God with having the very worst character of any being in the universe. For when we take into consideration God's promises and declarations, how can we possibly exercise unbelief without virtually charging Him with the very opposite of all His promises and professions.

Consider again the illustration of the student, whose father has by letter repeatedly assured him that all his needs would be supplied. Now if these assurances were complete, often repeated, and even backed by an oath, it is clear to see this son could not doubt or be uneasy about his temporal support without calling into question his father's ability or willingness to provide for him. Suppose that the father has made as many, and great, and varied promises as God has; and has made as great a sacrifice to promote the well-being of his son, as God has to promote our well-being—could anything be conceived more injurious to the father's feelings and character than for the son to manifest no confidence in his father's word?

Unbelief has the most injurious capability of any sin in the world:

(1) To ourselves, unbelief renders all heart-obedience impossible. How can we obey God from the heart when we have no confidence in Him? All obedience to any authority, parental or state government, or to the moral government of God, implies and must necessarily be based upon confidence in the ruler. If private or public confidence is destroyed, to the same degree is the obedience of the heart rendered impossible.

(2) Unbelief is in its tendency the most injurious sin among men that can be conceived. It is a most contagious abomination. How easily unbelief prevailed over our first parents when the serpent suggested to Eve that God was not sincere in His prohibition. It is truly remarkable to witness its contagion. Let anyone suggest a question or doubt, or manifest in his conduct that he has no confidence in God and His promises, and the influence seems to go forth almost with the power of omnipotence. If professing Christians manifest by their careless lives their unbelief in the guilt and danger of sinners, it seems to promote an immunity in them toward the warnings in God's Word. The most solemn assertions and threatenings are not regarded by them as anything more than the baseless fabrication of a dream. I have often been astonished to see how mere hints of unbelief can chill everything to death, and quench the spirit of prayer and confidence in God in revival meetings. Let anyone but suggest, under such circumstances, that the revival is going to decline; that God cannot work, because certain things prevent Him; let him but call into question the application or meaning of the promises, and it will be seen how easily confidence can be destroyed. Unbelief in any case, if it finds vent, will spread in a community like a floodtide.

Unbelief tends to annihilate God's influence on the earth. His influence on the mind consists in the estimation in which He is held by moral beings. Wherever there is not a felt confidence in God, His influence over that mind is destroyed. Hereby unbelief tends to the complete nullification of the government of God. One great design of the atonement was to restore public confidence. Satan suggested, and our first parents believed him, that God was selfish in prohibiting their eating a certain fruit, on the ground that they would "become as Gods, knowing good and evil." The atonement further intended to exhibit in the strongest manner God's disinterested love to people, that He might restore their confidence in Him, and thus gain dominion over their hearts for their good and His own glory.

In the atonement He has given the highest evidence that He possibly could give of the disinterested nature and infinite degree of His love. Unbelief succeeds in setting all this aside, and declares that it has no confidence whatever in God. Thus it renders ineffective the power of moral government and makes the gospel a savor of death unto death. It is a direct refusal to be satisfied with the infinite evidence that God has given of His unconditional love for people. It is virtually saying, "I will not be satisfied with any evidence that God has given or can give of the integrity of His character. He is not to be trusted. He shall not have my confidence, say or do what He may."

Unbelief is the most grievous sin against God of any that can be committed. Suppose a husband should find that his wife had no confidence at all in him, though he has displayed to her the sincerest affection, manifesting it in every possible way. Now what could be more grievous to his heart than to find that his wife had no confidence in him?

If, under these circumstances, a husband is put to grief, and justified to feel deeply injured and wounded to the very heart; what must be the state of God's feelings when He sees that His creatures have no confidence in Him in spite of the infinite pains He has taken to secure their confidence and thereby save their souls? Unbelief tramples the Son of God underfoot, and counts the blood of the covenant an unholy thing, wherewith he has sanctified mankind, and does despite to the Spirit of grace. Unbelief says, "I have no confidence in the necessity, the nature, or the reality of the Atonement; and as for Jesus Christ, I do not believe that 'His blood cleanseth from all sin.' I do not feel in my heart that He is 'my wisdom, and righteousness, and sanctification, and redemption.' In fact, I do not knowingly believe any such thing."

Unbelief is at the root of all other sins. A little reflection on the subject will convince anyone that unbelief, or the withholding of confidence in the character of God, His word and promises, is the central cause of worldly mindedness and selfishness manifested in so many forms in the world today. Let the mind but have a conscious assurance that all the Bible is true and reliable, and it instantly breaks the power of selfishness, pride, and every other abomination, and delivers the soul up to the entire dominion of truth.

Unbelief sets aside infinite evidence, and therefore, is the greatest conceivable departure from the law of our nature. I have already remarked that belief in testimony is natural to man; and the mind in an unperverted state is as yielding as air to the influence of evidence. But what must be the state of that mind that can withhold confidence in God in the face of all the evidence He has given of the infinite excellence of His character. It is the most outrageous mutiny against the laws of our being, the most abominable setting at nought and turning upside down of all the tendencies of the unperverted mind that can be conceived.

Unbelief is the most horrible exhibition of prejudice that the world anywhere presents or ever witnessed. But for the appalling display of the facts in the case, it would seem utterly incredible that people should not be entirely satisfied, and exercise the most implicit confidence in the character of God, His word and promises.

We sometimes witness very shocking exhibitions of prejudice in human beings toward one another, insomuch that the prejudiced mind can really believe nothing good of him against whom the prejudice is entertained. Whatever appears to be fair, he suspects of hypocrisy, and accounts for any appearance of goodness in any way except to admit the reality. Everyone would probably agree that there are few more hateful exhibitions of the human character than this. But how infinitely detestable is the state of mind that is so given up to prejudice against God, as to at once set aside the infinite weight of testimony in His favor, and to withhold all practical and heartfelt confidence in His word and oath?

God has done all that the nature of the case requires to secure and even compel the exercise of confidence in Him. Imagine some mischievous mind that introduces rebellion into a human government by insinuations that destroy the confidence of the people in their ruler. And suppose that while the ruler has the power to overcome, crush, and slay all the offenders, he in spite of this so pities them as to give his only son to atone for their sins. Further suppose that while every exhibition of his unconditional love is made, yet confidence is withheld, and his revolted subjects continue to maintain their pernicious distrust in his character.

Well might the ruler ask, "What more could I have done than I have to secure the confidence of this people? I have forfeited the life of my son to redeem you, and how is it that you do not believe?" One might think it impossible that unbelief could thrive in a world resplendent with all the manifestations of God's love. But what can we say, when we find not only the heathen world, but the Christian world and even the Christian Church, lacking confidence in God and manifesting the most shocking unbelief in regard to His providence and Word? What more can God do to secure public and individual confidence? What higher evidence can He give? Or, in His own emphatic language, "What more can I do for my vineyard than I have already done?"

Unbelief is eminently a willful sin. It is a matter of common observation that it is exceedingly hard to make people believe what they are unwilling to believe. And when the will is strongly opposed to any truth it is next to impossible to retain the confidence of the mind in that truth. But what must be the strength of depravity in that heart, what must be the power of prejudice, what invincible strength must there be in the opposition of that will, when the confidence of the mind is not secured by concrete evidence; when the mind can look over the whole field and see mountains of evidence, and yet not feel a particle of inward confidence and peace of heart in the character and word of the blessed God.

The influence of the will in modifying our belief, on almost any subject, can be strikingly illustrated in a great many ways. A drunkard does not *believe* that alcohol is poison. A Universalist does not *believe* that there is any hell.

An epicure does not *believe* that his non-nutritious condiments are injurious to his health. A tea or coffee drinker will not *believe* that those substances could be injurious. And it is often striking to observe the amount of influence the will has in modifying the opinions of men. And when we come to speak of the faith of the gospel, which implies and includes volition, it is self-evident that there can be no faith where the will does not yield. To talk of an unwilling faith is to speak of an unwilling willingness. The truth is that people are not influenced by evidence in cases where their will is opposed to the truth. They are stubborn and rebellious, not convinced, not humbled, and their confidence is not gained, no matter what God says.

Let me conclude with several comments.

First, one unbelieving soul may do an immense amount of evil; especially if he is a minister of the gospel! How easy it is for a blind minister to keep his congregation forever in darkness with regard to the meaning of the gospel and the fullness of the salvation provided. A mind under the influence of unbelief is a very dangerous interpreter of the Word of God. Without faith, no one discovers the true meaning of the Bible. Nor can he by any possibility discover its spiritual import, without that state of mind which is always implied in a right understanding of the Word of God.

The Church is robbed of its inheritance by unbelief. Inasmuch as the promises are conditioned upon faith, and cannot in their own nature be fulfilled where there is not faith, how far-reaching is the evil of unbelief in the Church of God? Gospel rest and salvation lie before them in all their fullness, completeness of Christian character in Christ Jesus and the sanctification of body, soul, and spirit are proffered to them and urged with infinite sincerity upon them; but all are rejected through unbelief. Those who are unbelieving in regard to the fullness of Christ's salvation take away the key of knowledge. They neither enter into gospel rest themselves, and those that would enter they hinder. Especially is this true of those ministers who call in question the attainability of entire consecration to God in this life. Unbelief is the last sin that deserves any commiseration, and yet it is very generally whined over, as if it were a calamity rather than a crime.

An unlearned but spiritual mind will understand the Bible much more readily than learned unbelief. A spiritual mind is learned in spiritual things. One may know much about other things, and have no spiritual discernment in respect to the truth of God. It is distressing to see a person who thinks himself learned look with a degree of contempt upon the opinions of those whom he considers unlearned in respect to the real meaning of the Bible.

Faith sees the doctrine of entire sanctification abundantly revealed in the Word of God. And when once the attention of the mind is directed to the examination of this question, it has often appeared remarkable to me that anyone should doubt whether this is a doctrine of revelation. I have already remarked upon the inference which Paul drew, from the last verses of the sixth chapter of 2 Corinthians: "And what agreement hath the temple of God with idols? For ye are the temple of the living God; as God hath said, I will dwell in them and walk in them; and I will be their God, and they shall be my people. Wherefore come out from among them, and be ye separate, saith the Lord, and touch not the unclean thing; and I will receive you, and will be a Father unto you, and ye shall be my sons and daughters, saith the Lord Almighty." Now the faith of Paul instantly recognized in these promises, which he quoted from the Old Testament, the truth that entire sanctification is attainable in this life; and immediately adds, "Having therefore these promises, dearly beloved, let us cleanse ourselves from all filthiness of the flesh and spirit, perfecting holiness in the fear of God."

Here, then, Paul saw a sufficient guarantee for the belief of this doctrine, and that to "perfect holiness in the fear of God," was, by the grace of God, put entirely within our reach. Now if Paul could draw such an inference as this from these promises, (and who, when they consider what is implied in the promises, can say that his inference was not legitimate?) what shall we say of that person who can look over all the exceeding great and precious promises which have been given that we might be made partakers of the divine nature, and yet see nothing to inspire the confidence that a state of entire sanctification in this life is in such a sense attainable, as to make its attainment a reasonable object of pursuit?

No one rightly understands and believes the Bible who is living in the indulgence of any known sin. Multitudes seem to be trying to maintain a state of spirituality, while in some things and perhaps in many, they are not entirely upright in their lives. They do not walk according to the best light they have, and are yet trying to exercise faith and keep up spiritual fellowship with God. The thing is naturally and forever impossible. Spiritual mindedness and disobedience are direct contraries. It is absurd to expect to have communion with God and yet live in the indulgence of any known sin.

Many think they have faith who are yet conscious that they have no inward, felt confidence or assurance of mind in regard to the Word and promises of God. They are not conscious of doubt or disbelief in what God has said; but are in that state of mind, that, while it does not deny directly and consciously, yet has no felt, practical confidence in the truth of God.

The lowest degree of real faith has, for a long time, been looked upon as a rare attainment in piety. That state of mind in which a person feels a confident assurance that God's promises shall be fulfilled and that views the truth of God as a reality, has been looked upon, and spoken of, as evidencing a high degree of spirituality; when, in fact, such a state of mind is essential to the exercise of real faith. In view of this subject, and of the present state of the Church, it is no wonder that Christ inquired, "When I come shall I find *faith* upon the earth?"

No one truly believes who finds it hard to love. True "faith works by love." Love is the natural and certain result of living faith.

No one truly believes who finds it hard to repent. Can he find it difficult to repent of his sins, who sees the death of Christ to be a reality?

No one believes who has not the spirit of thanksgiving and praise. Multitudes of individuals suppose themselves to believe, who rarely, if ever, are exercised with a spirit of thanksgiving and of praise to God. Can it be possible that any mind can believe, and have a realizing sense of the infinite love, truth and grace of God, and yet have no heart to praise Him? No one believes who finds it difficult to pray. Can a person who has a realizing sense of the state of the world and of the Church, and of the willingness and ability of God to bless people, be restrained in prayer?

Will not his very breath be prayer, devotion, and praise? Will not his very heart within him be melted? Will not his heart of compassion yearn mightily over a dying world?

And will not his soul stand in a continual attitude of thanksgiving, praise and supplication?

3

BLESSEDNESS OF BENEVOLENCE

"It is more blessed to give than to receive" (Acts 20:35b).

On what occasion our Lord Jesus Christ uttered these words we are not informed, since they are not recorded by the Evangelists. But we have the authority of an inspired apostle that He taught this doctrine. In considering this subject I will state what constitutes true Christianity, some of the elements that enter into the happiness of the true Christian, and notice several forms of delusion under which many are laboring.

What constitutes true Christianity:

The whole of Christianity may be comprehended in the simple term, benevolence or love. This love must be supreme in degree toward God and equal to other people.

It must also be disinterested.

This means that God must be loved for what He is, and our neighbor's happiness must be chosen and sought for its own sake, and not from any interested or selfish motive. But I must enter still more particularly into what is implied in benevolence, or that love which constitutes Christianity. It implies a spirit of justice, of mercy, of truth, of contentment

51

in goodness. of opposition to sin, and sinners as such. These are only some of the modifications of benevolence as it is developed by circumstances calling for these particular expressions of it. But benevolence, in general, implies a desire to promote the happiness of all beings—an expression of *good will*, promoting the express happiness of its object. In a still more extended sense, it is the love of being, promoting happiness for its own sake. It regards the happiness of every being that is capable of it as a substantial and genuine good in itself, and desires his happiness most who has the greatest capacity for it. It implies, also, a desire to promote the happiness of enemies as well as friends. True benevolence does not distinguish in this respect between enemies and friends, but regards the happiness of all as a valid good. Happiness is its object, and whether this can be promoted in an enemy or a friend, it matters not.

Benevolence not only implies a *desire*, but the *choice* of the happiness of all beings, so far as it can be consistently promoted. It is very common for people to desire things which, upon the whole, they do not choose, the desires or emotions often being in opposition to the will. It should be understood that benevolence is *good willing* and not merely good desiring. People's desires do not influence their outward conduct any further than their will is in accordance with their desires. Good willing always produces good acting, because the will always governs the external conduct; but there may be much desire that never begets corresponding action. The benevolence that constitutes true Christianity is a *disposition* of the mind, in distinction from those unintentional choices that are sometimes made under the pressure of peculiar circumstances, which after all, by no means constitute the character of a person.

A miser may be so wrought upon, and his constitutional susceptibilities so excited by the presence of some object of great distress, as for the moment to open his hand to give relief, and perhaps in five minutes call himself a thousand fools for having done so. No one therefore would say that this was true benevolence. It implies no radical change in his character. It is only the wringing from his selfish hand, by the force of circumstances acting on his constitutional susceptibilities, what it was not in his heart to give, and that which would not have been given, but as a relief to his own agony at the time.

Understand that the benevolence which constitutes true Christianity is a continually abiding disposition of the mind. I mean by disposition what is commonly meant by it, the controlling propensity of a person's mind. We speak of a person as having an avaricious disposition, a worldly, jealous, or envious disposition. We call this a disposition, because we observe it to be the permanent bent or tendency of the mind. The avaricious person manifests his disposition in all his worldly arrangements. It is seen to be the great tendency and effort of his mind to gain worldly possessions. The envious man is seen to be instituting comparisons between himself and others, and naturally and always to manifest an ill temper toward those whom he considers as competitors or superiors.

Now a benevolent person is seen to have a benevolent disposition. That is his manifest character. The happiness of being is the great object of pursuit with him. He lays his plans of doing good, and of carrying out and gratifying his leading disposition, just as naturally and certainly as an avaricious person would. But while the avaricious person lays his plans to get and hoard up, the benevolent person lays his plans to diffuse abroad. All others are aiming under some form to promote self-interest, to promote their own happiness by direct efforts. But the benevolent person seeks not his own happiness, but finds it in endeavoring to make others happy. His own happiness is not the object of pursuit. And yet he is the more certain to find it in proportion as he has the less regard to it.

To illustrate this: suppose that two men are accosted by a miserable beggar in circumstances of the utmost necessity. One of them is a selfish and the other a benevolent man.

They are both exercised however with a degree of compassion and both give of their means to the object of distress. It is easy to see that he is the most happy in giving who is the most disinterested, and who has the least regard to his own happiness in the case, because the relief to the other is to him the greatest gratification. If real piety and true benevolence were the sole motives that induced the benevolent man to give, the relief of the beggar would beget in him unmingled satisfaction, while at the same time, the one who was less benevolent would feel less intent on relieving his necessities, and of course less gratified and less happy by witnessing the relief. Understand, then, and always bear in mind, that Christian benevolence is a controlling disposition, or propensity of mind, and develops itself just as any other disposition manifests itself, by the daily walk of its possessor.

Elements of happiness:

Happiness consists in the *exercise* of benevolence itself. The human mind is so constructed by its Creator that the exercise of benevolence in itself is exceedingly sweet and gratifying to the mind. It has an excellent relish and warmth that enters into the very substance of the exercise. There is a conscious happiness diffused through the mind that seems to be woven into the very texture of benevolence itself.

This is to the benevolent mind like the perennial fountain pouring forth continually the sweet and refreshing waters of life. Another element of Christian happiness is that which consists in the gratification of the benevolent disposition. I have already said there is a sweet satisfaction in the *exercise* itself. But still, the exercise is one thing and its gratification another. The gratification is another ingredient that greatly augments the sum of happiness. To will to do good is sweet, but to really succeed in doing the good that we desire is sweeter still.

Included in the whole of the Christian's happiness is the satisfaction that follows and accompanies the exercise or gratification of benevolence. This is indispensable to complete happiness. <u>People may experience a kind and degree of happiness in indulging in those things in which all the powers of the mind do not harmonize; but if they are indulging in things to which their consciences are opposed, the inward mutiny and conflict thus produced mingles in their cup of gratification the gall of bitterness.</u> But benevolence always has the approbation of conscience. And the mind, from its very structure, necessarily feels a genuine satisfaction in the exercise of benevolent affections.

Still another portion of this happiness is the life and harmonious action of all the powers of the soul in its exercise. The mind is so constructed that it will not and cannot harmonize in any other course of action. It was made to be benevolent. Benevolence is its proper element, and it can no more properly enjoy life in the exercise of selfish affections than a fish can live out of water. But there is an excellent harmony, like an exquisitely tuned instrument, in the movements of all the powers of the mind in the exercise and gratification of benevolence. Like an exquisite machine, intricately made, and kept clean and oiled so as to cut off all friction as far as is possible, so benevolence moves as smoothly, sweetly, safely—there is a loveliness in the harmony of its movements. And the soul in the exercise of benevolence is made to harmonize. Every power of the mind consents. There is no jarring, no grating, no friction, no inward mutiny or repellancy to cause discord; but all is loveliness, quietness and assurance forever.

Probably an even stronger element of the Christian's happiness is the full assurance that he pleases God. The mind is so constructed that when it is conscious of exercising perfect benevolence, it can no more doubt that it pleases God than it can doubt its own existence. Love naturally and necessarily casts out all fear. There is in the very workings of benevolence itself the accompanying assurance that these affections and this course of conduct please God.

Together with the happiness derived from knowing that

one pleases God is the joy and rejoicing in the happiness God himself experiences. Remember, the happiness of being is the benevolent person's object of pursuit. He rejoices in true happiness wherever he sees it, and even greater satisfaction is gained when he contemplates a greater existence of it. To him the happiness of God is infinitely the greatest good in the universe, and the glory of God, as it stands connected with the happiness of God and that of His whole government, is considered by him as the supreme good.

The consideration then of God's infinite, eternal happiness and glory is the source of present, perpetual, and eternal consolation. What a consideration for a benevolent mind to dwell upon is the endless, unchanging happiness of God: a fathomless, shoreless ocean of perfect blessedness. To a benevolent mind this is an unfailing source of eternal joy.

A further source of the Christian's happiness is the happiness and good of all other beings. A truly benevolent mind participates in and really enjoys the happiness that exists all around him, as if it were his own. Nothing can prevent a benevolent mind from tasting the cup of every man's happiness and sharing with every man the happiness of those good things which God bestows upon him, without in the least degree diminishing the bliss of him whose happiness he shares. He is entirely satisfied and rejoices to see things bestowed upon others that are withheld from himself. If, in time of great drought, for example, a cloud arises that promises rain to water his farm, his garden, or his neighborhood, and if a change of wind carries the blessing to another town, where it is as much needed, he is equally well pleased and enjoys the refreshing of his neighbors as if it were his own.

A Christian derives happiness through his direct personal efforts to promote the good of others. His very toil and labor have in them the relish of sweetness, and carry with them and in them their own reward. A benevolent mind *is* a disposition to do good to others. And because he is acting from his own disposition, while he is not *seeking* his happiness as an end at all, he is surely *finding* an exquisite enjoyment in his disinterested efforts to do good.

The Christian's happiness consists in the present and eternal indulgence of a ruling tendency or disposition to do good. He really has nothing more important to do, anymore than God has, and from the very moment of his conversion to all eternity, he has but to pursue uninterruptedly and as zealously as he pleases, the ruling disposition of his soul. God further arranges circumstances so as to surround him continually with objects upon which he can gratify his benevolence. He has an ample field for the exercise and pouring out of all the benevolence of his soul in efforts to do good.

Several forms of delusion.

Many seem to mistake *light* for Christian faith.

They get some new views of religious truth which produce a corresponding excitement of mind, and they bustle about under the impression that this enthusiasm is Christian faith. If they would take an honest look, it would be seen that their heart is still selfish, and not benevolent; that their ruling propensity or disposition is not changed; that while they are excited by their new views of religions truth, it is *emotion* and not *will* that is active. Their business habits and transactions will soon reveal the fact that selfishness is after all, in some form, the ruling tendency of their mind. In all such cases, there is of course a radical mistake, a fatal delusion, under which the mind is laboring.

Many are deceiving themselves by the exercise of a legal religious zeal. Paul testified of his countrymen, that "they had a zeal of God, but not according to knowledge." I have long been convinced that much of the zeal manifested by those who profess to be Christians and by many professed converts is of this character. They slumber on, until awakened by the thunders of the Law and judgment; then they bluster about, urged by a sense of duty and conscience, and a multitude of legal considerations while they are fully aware that they are not influenced by the deep love of God and of souls. The evidences of such a legal spirit are: (1) An evident lack of a deeply heart-broken and humble spirit. (2) An evident lack of a deep satisfaction of mind in the work itself. (3) The absence of that abiding soul satisfaction which belongs to the exercise and gratification of benevolence.

Many very zealous persons are anything but truly happy in the exercise of the affections which are working within them. They carry with them all the while a sense of condemnation. They feel as if their holiest exercises need to be confessed as sins, and there is all the while a grating and friction within, a felt consciousness that all is not right, a sense of defilement, a lack of integrity and uprightness of intention, and a consciousness of selfish motives in everything they say or do.

People in this state of mind do not conceive what a clean heart is. They do not understand the immense and radical difference between their feelings and the exercises of a purely benevolent mind. How a person can live without condemnation, they cannot understand. And their experience being what it is, they obviously look with great suspicion upon any who profess to live without a sense of condemnation. They judge, of course, that it is because they are not well acquainted with their own hearts, and also are ignorant of the purity of God's law. Now I can understand very well, from my own experience, what this state of mind is. I know very well what it is to have a legal zeal that would compass land and sea to make a proselyte, and yet carry with it, as if woven into its very texture, the sense of condemnation. The fact is, the mind is so constructed that whenever it is enlightened, it cannot be satisfied with a legal zeal. Nothing but the exercise of unmixed benevolence can make it happy. Nothing but a conscious exercise of right affections can free it from the sting of self-condemnation.

Herein is a vast delusion. People with a purely legal zeal are very apt to suppose that there is no other state than this to which Christians may attain in this life, and thus they judge, censure, and condemn all who profess the consciousness of a clean heart. Many mistake emotion for disposition. They do not distinguish between the emotions which constitute their excitement of mind and that controlling disposition, or state of the will, that constitutes true benevolence.

Others will mistake mere assent for a right disposition. They are enlightened, and hold correct opinions. They also know that Christianity is not made up of emotion, and are satisfied without any of it. They do not take into consideration that although emotions may sometimes exist independent of the will, they flare up most easily in accordance with it. People feel more deeply about that which motivates their minds. Therefore, if an individual supposes that he has a benevolent disposition, but his emotions are not readily activated in the presence of obvious need, he is deceived. He has the religion of opinion, and not a ruling disposition.

There are many instances in which individuals are deceived by attributing to benevolence that which is actually only one form of selfishness triumphing over another. For example:

(1) The love of reputation may be the supreme ruling propensity of mind, able to triumph over lust, intemperance and a host of other subordinate tendencies. A man or a woman may be liberal in giving, chaste in conversation and deportment, and of temperate habits, and all this may be accredited to true benevolence, when in fact, it should be ascribed to the love of reputation.

(2) A literary ambition may succeed in depressing sloth or inordinate appetite, as well as other evil, but subordinate, propensities of the mind.

(3) A spirit of avarice may be the ruling tendency of the mind, and triumph over lust, intemperance and many forms of sin.

(4) Selfish fears and hopes may restrain inward wickedness, simply displacing sin with other forms of it.

All these restraints may be, and often are, imagined to be a result of pure benevolence, when in fact they are only one form of selfishness, controlling and subordinating other forms of the same principle. The only remaining form of delusion, that I shall now address, is that which results from the individual's happiness consisting not in the exercise of his benevolence, but in the consideration of his own safety. We sometimes see persons settle down into an Antinomian security, and manifest great quietness and peace of mind where happiness and peace are manifestly based upon the consideration of their own safety. Now this is as far as possible from a truly Christian state of mind. Real Christian happiness arises out of the exercise of Christianity itself. It is the exercise or gratification of benevolence, with its necessary accompaniments, that constitutes the happiness of the true saint. To be sure, the contemplation of the grace of Christ, the joys of heaven, and an eternity of blessedness at God's right hand come in to make up the aggregate of a Christian's happiness; but the basis and foundation of the whole is that which belongs to the exercise and resulting satisfaction of benevolent action.

The natural heart does not apprehend the true nature of Christian faith. I have often wondered what skeptics can be thinking about, and how it is that they can have any doubts of the necessity of a change of heart. But a consideration of the selfishness of their hearts explains the whole difficulty. God's state of mind is the exact opposite of their own. Benevolence is the contrast of a selfish disposition. Selfishness finds its happiness in getting; benevolence in giving. Selfishness is always endeavoring to promote its own, and benevolence the happiness of others.

This remark leads me to say that we can see the necessity of examples to illustrate the true nature of Christianity. One of the leading objectives of Christ's taking upon himself human nature was to associate with human beings, and reveal to their minds the true idea of God's character; so to live and associate with them that they might observe how God would conduct himself as a neighbor, brother, son, or friend; what spirit and temper He possessed and would manifest under the circumstances in which people find themselves.

As soon as a few had caught the revelation that God was love, He sent them forth, "as sheep among wolves," to lay down their lives, as He had done, for a rebellious world. They caught His spirit, imitated His example, and the waves of salvation rolled wherever they went; and a few years had well nigh seen a world prostrate at the feet of Christ. But alas! the world, with her selfish and polluting embrace, soon seduced the Church into selfishness and apostasy from God. And the world can never be converted, unless examples and illustrations of what true Christianity is are held up in the lives of professing Christians before the eyes of men.

You can see from this subject what constitutes real apostasy from God. The moment you set up a selfish interest as the object of pursuit, go anywhere, engage in any business, marry, or take any other step inconsistent with the exercise and pursuit of the will of God, you are in a state of apostasy. You have forsaken the fountain of living waters and are "hewing out broken cisterns that can hold no water."

You can also visualize what constitutes the happiness of God. Benevolence is His whole character. His benevolence is infinite. His happiness is, therefore, infinite and unchangeable. We have shown that Christians may and ought to be as happy in proportion to their capacity as God is.

Likewise we see what determines the unhappiness of many professing Christians. It is selfishness—it is naturally impossible for a selfish mind to be happy. Selfishness releases a brood, as it were, of scorpions and vipers to sting the soul's happiness to death.

So we see what constitutes the misery of humanity without Christ. They are pressing after happiness but cannot obtain it, the reason being that they are seeking it where it cannot truly exist. If a person pursues his own happiness as an end, he may as well expect to eliminate his own shadow. The mind is so created that happiness cannot possibly be obtained in this way. To exercise kindness without hope of reward is the only possible way to be happy. To seek not your own, but another's good, is forever and unalterably indispensable to the happiness of a moral being.

What striking evidence does the human constitution afford of the benevolence of God! He has so constructed it that happiness is the certain and necessary result of benevolence, and that no other possible working of the constitution can result in happiness. What striking and unanswerable testimony is this to the benevolence of the Author of our nature!

Those who do not enjoy the good things of others, nor find reason to be thankful for blessings bestowed upon others, are not Christians. I have already said that true benevolence is the love or desire for our neighbor's happiness, even choosing his happiness over our own. Whenever blessings are conferred upon others, we are truly pleased. It is what we desire most. It is in harmony with the ruling tendency of our minds. It is just as certain as our very existence that, if we are benevolent, we shall rejoice with them that rejoice, and weep with them that weep; that we shall participate in the joys and sorrows of those around us, and rejoice in and be thankful for all the good bestowed upon the world.

From these observations it is easy to see of what spirit those are who readily murmur at others possessing good things, of which they themselves are deprived. Did you ever observe a family of selfish children, and witness their complainings and murmurings whenever something was bestowed upon one, and not on the others: "But, Mother, you have given my brother such and such and have not given it to me. Why not let me have the best things; let me have the largest piece, the most and best of everything?" This is a supremely hateful spirit; but it is exactly the spirit of many professing Christians. Instead of rejoicing to see their brothers and sisters blessed with temporal or spiritual good things, they are ready to murmur and be offended because these things are not bestowed on them. This manifests the supreme selfishness of their minds, and affords the highest demonstration that they are not Christians.

They also cannot be Christians who have no heart to thank God for bestowing blessings upon their enemies. There is no Christian faith in selfish gratitude. A supremely selfish individual may well be thankful for blessings bestowed upon himself, or upon his close friends, who are accounted as parts of himself. But a truly benevolent person will rejoice in blessings bestowed on his enemies as well as his friends.

It is easy to see that the covetous and the selfishly ambitious are not and cannot be Christians; that a spirit of worldly competition is utterly inconsistent with the spirit of benevolence.

What must that state of mind be that is never willing to do a neighbor a kindness without taking pay for it? Some people never seem to have the spirit of doing good, or of obliging anyone but themselves. Payment seems to be the sole motive for doing almost anything and everything for those around them. They seem never to enjoy the luxury of making those around them happy for its own sake. And if they do anything for a neighbor, it is, by no means, for the sake of doing good, but for the remuneration they may receive.

Now, if a minister of the gospel should be actuated by such motives in visiting the sick, and in preaching the gospel, everyone would say there was no virtue in it. They go to visit the sick as often as the physician, making as much effort to restore the health of the soul as the other does the body, and in all this they are expected to be actuated by pure benevolence. They would never think of asking for payment, whether they receive a salary or not. What minister has not traveled hundreds of miles, and spent hours, and days, and weeks, and months in such labors of love without ever expecting or desiring to receive an earthly remuneration for it? He has found in the very exercise itself an excellent solace, an exquisite relish, that was to his benevolent mind worth more than gold.

Surely what is expected of ministers of the gospel in this respect should be true of all Christians. They should as far as possible "do good and lend, hoping for nothing again." They should be actuated by disinterested benevolence, knowing that "with whatsoever measure they mete it shall be measured to them again." And what is the motive of those who are unwilling to exercise any self-denial for the sake of doing good to others? There are those who will not give up what is called the temperate use of alcohol for the sake of his brothers. He contends that it is lawful for *him* to use it moderately; that others have no right to make a stumbling block of his use of it; and as for practicing self-denial for the sake of example, he will not do it.

There may be a woman who professes to love God supremely and her neighbor as herself. She prays for the heathen and thinks herself truly religious; and yet, she will not deny herself the use of tea and coffee or some other luxury to save a heathen world from hell. The cry of eight hundred million human souls is coming upon every wind of heaven, calling out, "send us tracts; send us Bibles; send us missionaries; send us the means of eternal life; for we are dying in our sins."

"Oh, but," say these professing Christians, "times are hard; money is scarce; we are in debt; we must turn away our ears from hearing these wailings of woe." Now brother, sister, let me sit down at your table.

What have you here? How much does this tea and coffee cost you a year? How much do these worse than useless articles of luxury curtail your ability to send the gospel to the perishing? My sister, how many scriptures and tracts have you denied the lost in this way? How many Bibles, at five shillings each, might be sent to the heathen every year, were you but willing to exercise a little self-denial, and that which as well might benefit your own health and highest good?

Brother, perhaps you use tobacco. How long have you used it? What does it cost you a year? How many heathen might this day have had Bibles in their hands for the price of your habit, who will now go to hell, without ever hearing of the Savior—who might have heard of eternal life, had you possessed some benevolence in your heart? Will you make the calculation? Will you ask yourself how many Bibles and tracts might have been purchased with the money you have squandered? Will you settle the question, once and for all, whether you are truly influenced by the love of God and of souls? And whether you eat and drink and enjoy these things for the glory of God, or for the gratification of your own pleasures? Surely, the question is of no less importance than whether benevolence or selfishness constitutes your character.

For many, Christian responsibilities are not a source of the highest enjoyment to them. In fact, the Christianity of many persons seems to make them miserable, and whatever they do for the cause of Christ they seem to do painfully and grudgingly. The reason is, they are not motivated by love. If love were the ruling disposition of their hearts, their walk of faith would be a source of sweet enjoyment to them. There are those who prefer getting to giving for the cause of Christ. The truly benevolent will value property, only as the means of promoting the cause upon which their heart is set.

Everything is esteemed by them in proportion as it relates to and bears upon the Kingdom of Christ. Life, health, time, property, talents—everything is brought into the service of God, and regarded only as the means of promoting His glory and the good of souls. A truly benevolent mind places no value upon money for its own sake. He no more desires to hoard up money to gratify and please himself than he would hoard up sticks and stones. In short, he places no earthly value upon money, or anything else, except as it can be made instrumental in doing good.

When, therefore, you see a person who loves to amass goods for himself, who is increasingly engaged in great business dealings, getting all he can for himself, and giving to the poor and to the cause of Christ only sparingly and with great effort, it is simple to affirm that he is a selfish, worldly man, and no Christian at all. In this connection you can see the delusion of that professing Christian who will be more zealous in seasons of speculative dealings, and enter with more enthusiasm into a money-making enterprise, than into a chance for investment in the cause of Christ. Great is the delusion of that professing Christian who more readily loses the spirit of revival than the spirit of speculation; in other words, whose religious zeal can be cooled down by an opportunity to make money, and who can be driven away from God and prayer by the opening of navigation, the coming in of the trading season, or when any new project of a lucrative nature becomes known to the public. There are many painful instances in which professors of religion will seem to bustle about and be active in religion at seasons of the year when they have little else to do, or when little can be done in business; but are ever ready to backslide, and are sure to do so, whenever an opportunity occurs to favor their own interests. But this is almost too plain a case of delusion to need remark.

In the light of this subject, you can see that there is no true spirituality without real benevolence of heart and life. Many people seem to be engaged in a most absurd attempt to keep up spirituality and a spirit of prayer and fellowship with God while they live and conduct their business upon principles of selfishness. Now nothing can be a greater insult to God than this: to pray for His Spirit, to attempt to have communion with Him, or even pretend to be His friend, while as a matter of fact selfishness is the rule of your life.

If "it is more blessed to give than to receive," what infinitely great satisfaction must God take in supporting so great a family. He is pouring out from His unlimited fullness an ocean of blessing continually. And what an infinite reward it must be to His benevolent mind to plan and execute all the good that He is promoting and will continue to do so into all eternity.

We see from these discussions how to understand the declaration concerning Christ: "that for the joy that was set before Him, He endured the cross, despising the shame, and is for ever set down at the right hand of God." Although multitudes of things connected with the atonement were in themselves painful, yet, upon the whole, the great work was a source of infinite satisfaction to the Father and the Son. God is virtuous in the atonement, in the same proportion as

He really enjoys the offering of it. "The Lord loveth a cheerful giver"; and we always regard that self-denial as most virtuous that is exercised most willingly. And where the greatest self-denial is exercised, not only with great willingness, but with great joyfulness for the sake of doing good to others, we pronounce that the highest degree of virtue. The Father is represented as being well pleased with the conduct of Christ in the atonement. He was greatly pleased with the virtue of His Son; to see Him count the work a joyous one in so freely and willingly denying himself to save His enemies from death.

If God finds it "more blessed to give than to receive," why should we not abound with every blessing that we need? Why should we, by our narrow-mindedness and unbelief, render it impossible for God to gratify His benevolent heart in giving us great things?

We see from this the secret of all unbelief in prayer. It comes from our own selfishness. I have already said that a selfish mind finds it difficult to conceive of the true character of God. A selfish man, knowing that he gives grudgingly, very naturally conceives of God as being such as he is. He finds it exceedingly difficult to grasp the fact, though rarely taught, that God is his exact opposite in this respect; that giving is His happiness; that He has infinitely more satisfaction in giving good things than we have in receiving them; that He has greater pleasure in giving things than the most avaricious man on earth has in getting. But it is no wonder that selfish minds are slow to understand and believe this.

There is no true religion but that which consists in union with the character of God, in being benevolent as He is benevolent, in having the same disposition—a settled, fixed, abiding disposition to benevolence. Study 1 John 4:7, 8, 16b: "Beloved, let us love one another: for love is of God; and every one that loveth is born of God, and knoweth God. He that loveth not, knoweth not God; for God is love. . . . And he that dwelleth in love dwelleth in God, and God in him."

4

A WILLING MIND, INDISPENSABLE TO A RIGHT UNDERSTANDING OF TRUTH

"If any man will do His will, he shall know of the doctrine, whether it be of God, or whether I speak of myself" (John 7:17).

In discussing this text I shall show that God's promises, with their conditions, are a revelation of the great principles of His government. There are several things that are implied in a willingness to do the will of God, and this state of mind is indispensable to a right understanding of the truth of God. Unless you tempt God by neglecting the means of knowledge, this state of mind will certainly result in a right knowledge of the truth.

God's promises, with their conditions, are a revelation of the great principles of His government.

God is unchangeable. What He does, or promises, or says at one time, He would do, or promise, or say, the circumstances being the same, at all times. Everything that He does and says is but a revelation of His character. He knows nothing of favoritism. His demonstrations of goodness are always founded in the reason, nature and relation of all things. He regards all beings and events according to their true nature, character and

69

relation to the whole. His providence, His threatenings, His law, gospel and promises, only reveal so many great, unchangeable principles of His government. And as He never changes, as there is in Him "no variableness or shadow of turning," we may rest with the utmost confidence in the fact that both a promise and its condition, that all the promises with their conditions, are founded in and are a revelation of the unalterable principles of His government.

Both the promise and the condition are founded in the nature and relation of all things. God always holds himself pledged to fulfill the same promises, under the same or similar circumstances, and upon the same conditions. These are irresistible inferences from His unchangeableness.

What is implied in a willingness to do His will.

It implies implicit confidence in His character. We should have no right to be willing to do the will of God, unless we had reason to confide in the perfection of His will. His character consists in the state of His will. To be willing, therefore, that His will should be done implies an unwavering confidence that His will is perfectly right. It implies the certain conviction on our part that He is absolutely omniscient, and knows perfectly what He ought to will, or what upon the whole is best to be done, and that His will is forever and unalterably just what it ought to be.

Willingness to do His will also implies supreme love to God. If any other being is loved more than He is, we should feel more desirous to please that being than to please God; for indeed that object, so loved, is in reality our God. A willingness therefore to do the will of God implies a supreme attachment to Him for His own sake, and the supreme desire of pleasing Him.

A supreme regard to God's authority is also here implied. It is absurd to say that we are willing to do His will, if our regard to His authority is not supreme. It is one thing to *desire* to do His will, and another thing to be *willing to do* it. It is a common thing for people to desire what, upon the whole, they do not choose. But to be *willing* to do God's will, instead of our own or that of any other being, certainly constitutes a supreme regard to His authority. We will also desire to do or to be wholly right or wholly conformed to the will of God.

It implies an intense desire and willingness to be right on every subject, to have our whole being and all the influences that we exert wholly and perfectly right, to be wholly conformed to the will of God in all the relations we sustain to Him and to the whole world in which we live, to have an intense desire and willingness to do and feel exactly right toward ourselves and all other beings.

It equally implies an intense desire and willingness to do our utmost to glorify God; to be consumed in His service, having every talent at his disposal, all time and every possession wholly devoted to the infinitely important end of glorifying God. God wills that we should be so; and a willingness to do His will implies an equal willingness in us to be so.

Our disposition should be to avoid whatever is displeasing to Him or contrary to His will, a willingness on our part to submit to any sacrifice, rather than displease Him. If a man would not sacrifice his own life, rather than knowingly displease God, he is not, in the sense of this text, willing to do His will.

Teachableness

Willingness at any cost to do His will requires a disposition to know the truth on all subjects, to be aware of what talent or ability He has given, how we can be best used in His Kingdom; what will contribute to the highest perfection of our body and soul, and to our greatest participation in His service. In short, it implies an earnest desire and readiness to know the whole circle of truth in relation to our whole being, all our responsibilities, all our influences, and all the will of God concerning us. If there remains a subject relating to the highest perfection of our bodies or souls, or our highest and best influence and usefulness, upon which we are unwilling to be enlightened, upon which we are not intensely desirous to be made aware, we cannot properly be said to be willing to do the will of God.

It implies that we have no passion or idol to spare or defend. But on the contrary, that we have wholly renounced idolatry under every form, and have cast off the dominion of fleshly desires, and are wholly devoted to the will of God.

It implies the renunciation of our own will, that we have no will except that God's will should be done. It implies the constant yielding up of our will to Him, and that the abiding state of our minds, and the constant echo of our hearts, is "Thy will—*thy* will—THY WILL, O God, be done."

We will no longer have any selfish interests to promote, for we have forever renounced all idea or desire of setting up any interest of our own as an end in itself, whether it be of temporal or eternal interest, material or spiritual. Further, "Whether we eat or drink, or whatsoever we do," we desire to promote "the glory of God."

It is implied in our commitment to the whole will of God that we have no longer any appetite or passion to consult or to defend, that we have no desire to pursue our own gratification in any respect as the sole end and object of life, and that no appetite or passion is indulged merely for the sake of the indulgence.

We must consider our whole being as God's, that our appetites were created to subserve the highest interests of our being, to be the servants and not the masters of our souls; and that, whether we eat or drink, sleep or wake, labor or rest, lie down or rise up, study or pray, preach or whatever we do, all is done from a supreme desire to do the will of God.

It implies that we have no reputation of our own to maintain or defend; but that, like our Master, we have made ourselves of no reputation. We must wholly renounce our reputation as of no value, except as connected with the kingdom of Christ. We must have so entirely given up our good name to Him as to be willing to have it cast out as evil. We must pray that anything that shall result with regard to our reputation will in the highest manner promote the ultimate glory of God.

We will have no longer any indulged prejudice to blind our minds, or harden our hearts, to prevent our knowing and doing the will of God. Prejudice is a state in which we make up our minds and commit ourselves before we are possessed of all the facts. To condemn an author before we have patiently and candidly examined and understood his views is a very common and injurious form of prejudice. To condemn a person or a sentiment without a most thorough examination and hearing of the whole manner is another odious form of prejudice. A willingness to do the will of God, therefore, implies the giving up of all prejudice on every subject, and an unreserved throwing of the mind open to conviction, to light, and truth with an entire readiness to follow the will of God in whatever direction it shall lead us.

The love of truth and of God will swallow up everything else, and come to be the ruling principle of our whole being— our meat, our drink, our life, to do the whole will of God. A knowledge of His will has, with our committed hearts, the power of omnipotence to sway our minds and carry us to all lengths in obedience to it.

We will have an honest and earnest disposition to be acquainted with all our errors of opinion and practice, a willingness to be searched with the utmost scrutiny; yea, with the scrutiny of omniscience itself, and we will feel the utmost gratitude to anyone who will point out to us anything in which we can, in any respect, be more perfectly conformed to the will of God.

When we fully desire His will in all things, we will have the greatest abhorrence of yielding over to Satan any part of our influence, time, talents, property, or anything whatever that should in any way thwart the will of God.

The state of mind which desires the will of God in all things is indispensable to a right understanding of the truth of God.

It is first a necessary state of mind because it promotes honesty and diligent inquiry. It is certain that you will never inquire honestly after truth unless you are willing to obey it.

You will not inquire diligently and perseveringly if you are not possessed of an intense desire to know and do the will of God. To suppose the contrary of this is manifestly absurd.

This state of mind is indispensable to a just appreciation of the value and force of evidence. Certainly it is ridiculous to say that a mind will justly appreciate the force of evidence, upon any subject of which it is not without reproach.

The frame of mind to which we have been referring is a prerequisite to the heart's embracing truth, when it is perceived by the intellect. It is not necessary to suppose that one already knows the truth about every subject in order to have a disposition to obey it. A mind may be in love with truth for its own sake. In this state it loves all truth upon all subjects. It goes forth with earnest longings in search of truth, and whenever and wherever it finds it, it receives and obeys it with all joyfulness. But unless the heart is in love with truth, it is not honest in the search of it, nor ready to embrace it when apprehended by the intellect.

It is impossible for the mind to receive the whole truth without this state of heart. Some shreds of truth may be perceived by the mind, and many things about it may be known, while the heart is in an unsubdued state. But the *whole truth* in all its intention, scope, and impact is never apprehended by an unsubmitted mind to the will of God.

This state of mind will certainly result in a right knowledge of the truth, unless you tempt God by rejecting the means of knowledge.

Tempting God may prevent the fulfillment of any promise where our own efforts are involved in the outcome. In the twenty-seventh chapter of Acts, we have an account of the shipwreck of Paul.

Here God expressly promised, through Paul, "that there should be no loss of any man's life among them, but of the ship." But when the sailors were about to abandon the ship, Paul informed them that if they did not remain on board their lives could not be saved. The promise was without any condition expressed; yet it implied of course that they should use the best means of which they were possessed to preserve their lives. For the sailors, therefore, to abandon the ship would be to tempt God. In which case, in spite of His promise, they would all be lost. Now it should be forever understood that where the conditions of a promise, either expressed or implied, are not complied with, we tempt God, and it is vain to expect their fulfillment.

We tempt God when we expect Him to violate the principles of His own government as revealed in His works, providence and Word. Example: if we neglect to use the means for the accomplishment of any end, and expect Him to bring it about by miracle, this is tempting God. Being less than honest, industrious and persevering than we ought to be in the search of truth is tempting God. We may expect to remain in ignorance. Restraining prayer on the subject of divine teaching is tempting God. He has expressly said to us, "If any man lack wisdom, let him ask of God, who giveth to all men liberally and upbraideth not, and it shall be given him." "Open your mouth wide and I will fill it." "Call unto me and I will answer thee, and show thee great and mighty things which thou knowest not."

The conditions upon which we are to be taught the will of God are expressly laid down in Proverbs 2:1–9: "My son, if thou wilt receive my words, and hide my commandments with thee; so that thou incline thine ear unto wisdom, and apply thine heart to understanding; yea, if thou criest after knowledge, and liftest up thy voice for understanding; if thou seekest her as silver, and searchest for her as for hid treasures; then shalt thou understand the fear of the Lord, and find the knowledge of God. For the Lord giveth wisdom: out of His mouth cometh knowledge and understanding. He layeth up sound wisdom for the righteous; He is a buckler to them that walk uprightly. He keepeth the paths of judgment, and preserveth the way of His saints. Then shalt thou understand righteousness, and judgment, and equity; yea, every good path."

Here are the conditions:

(1) A willingness to receive and treasure His words as of great importance.

(2) A willingness to incline the ear and apply the heart.

(3) A willingness to cry after knowledge and lift up the voice for understanding.

(4) An intenseness of desire to seek for her as silver, and search after her as for hid treasures.

Upon these conditions, it is added, "thou shalt understand the fear of the Lord and find the knowledge of God." To neglect any of these means, therefore, and then expect "to know the doctrine whether it be of God" is to tempt your Maker. If we fulfill the condition, we may expect the fulfillment of the promise. We shall surely have whatever truth is needful for us to know and as fast as we need to know it.

We are bound to feel assured of this. We are under just as much obligation to feel the inward assurance of it as we are to feel that God will not lie. If we are conscious that we fulfill the conditions, we have no right whatever to doubt. If we are conscious that we do not fulfill the conditions, we have no right to expect it. God will teach us as fast as He safely can. "He knows our frame and remembers that we are dust."

He knows how easily we are bewildered and overset with being taught too much at once. It is a well known truth that where children are taught too early and too fast, there is great danger of confusion or even illness. And so it is with us; God teaches us, if we are His children and are anxious to be taught, as fast as we are able to learn. He said to His disciples, "I have many things to say to you, but ye cannot bear them now." They were not spiritually mature enough to receive such knowledge. There needed to be a greater comprehension of certain truths and influence of the Holy Spirit upon their minds to prepare them for the reception of all that He desired to teach them.

If we are anxious to do the will of God in every area of

our lives, with a proper use of means at our disposal, we may expect His revelation on all subjects that relate to our greatest progress and usefulness in His service. We can expect direction with regard to our health and the right management of our bodies, restraint of its appetites and tendencies, how to keep it under and cause it to subserve the highest interests of the soul. In short, there is no subject of which we need knowledge, upon which we may not confidently expect Him to teach us all that we need to know in the diligent and honest use of means.

The opinions of a sensualist, or one under the dominion of his appetites and fleshly tendencies, are not to be trusted. He is prejudiced and uninterested in knowing the truth in relation to the self-denying gospel of Jesus Christ. His opinions on the subject of temperance and the true principles of physiological reform are not to be trusted for the same reason.

The opinions of a speculator or worldly minded man are not at all credible in respect to the application of the law of God to the business transactions of this world. He is not an expert upon this subject and remaining a speculator, cannot be an in impartial state of mind.

Very few persons have so renounced themselves as to be willing to know the whole truth in regard to all branches of reform. Likewise, few have renounced their fleshly appetites so as to be willing to know and do the truth upon the subject of their daily eating habits. Very few have so renounced self-interest as to be willing to embrace the truth concerning the subject of sanctification. He who has renounced himself will search for light, and greet and embrace it with great joy, in regard to every subject of life. He will find his soul panting after it with unutterable longings.

He who is willing to do the will of God will keep hard upon the heels of truth and practice it as fast as he can learn it. Truth upon any subject is his law. He no sooner sees than he obeys. His practice and his theory are at one. Many mistake the absence of resistance to the will of God, for actual willingness to do the will of God. There must be a heartfelt willingness, a longing of soul to know the whole truth. Without it, there is no actual willingness to do the will of God. We need not expect, as I have already intimated, that God will teach us all the truth at once. When Solomon prayed for wisdom and God informed him that he had given him his desire, it is not to be supposed that he felt at the time as if he had a great enlargement of wisdom. But wisdom was imparted as he had need of it. Soon after his request, and the assurance of God that his prayer was granted, the two women came to him with their controversy about the child, at which time wisdom equal to the occasion was imparted by God in accordance with His promise. So, in our own case, we are to rest assured that when we have need for knowledge, by faithful supplication to Him, and in the diligent use of means we shall surely be instructed.

From this subject it is easy to see that the trivial fault-finding of infidels against the Christian religion carry no weight. If they were really pious and holy men and gave evidence of being willing to know and do the will of God, they would know of the doctrine whether it be of God.

The same remark is applicable to Universalists. What confidence can be placed in their assertions in respect to the gospel of Christ?

Who does not know that as a body they are ungodly and unholy men?

God often teaches us in ways that greatly agonize and bewilder us at the time. When we pray for divine teaching, we should be entirely reconciled to letting God teach us in His own way, cost what it may, lest we tempt the Spirit of the Lord.

And now, beloved, are you in a receptive state of mind and are you willing to know and do the whole will of God in respect to your entire being? Are you willing to know and do your whole duty, and the whole truth, cost what it may, on all the great social issues that are before the public? Are you anxious to look into, to understand, to know and do all within your power on the subject of entire sanctification, abolition, temperance, moral reform? A man is very ill-informed who does not see that as certainly as we are made up of body and soul, spiritual and social reform are indispensable to permanent moral reform.

If a man is in a closed state of mind on any one subject, he will not know and thoroughly do his duty on the subject. He is in a frame of mind that forbids the reasonable expectation that he will. Beware then dearly beloved, I beseech you not to commit yourself on the wrong side of any question. I have greatly feared, and I may truly say that I have been troubled, lest many should do on the subject of entire sanctification, what others have done on the subjects of temperance and moral reform—so commit themselves against the truth as never to know of the doctrine whether it be of God.

And now let me, as I have often done, ask you to go down upon your knees and lay your whole heart open before the Lord. Beseech Him to search you and try your heart, and see whether you are wholly willing to conform your entire being to the will of God—to do, to say, to be nothing more or less than is for His glory. May the Lord give us grace to know and do His whole will.

5

THE GOSPEL, THE SAVOR OF LIFE OR OF DEATH

"Now thanks be unto God, which always causeth us to triumph in Christ, and maketh manifest the savour of his knowledge by us in every place. For we are unto God a sweet savour of Christ in them that are saved, and in them that perish: To the one we are the savour of death unto death; and to the other the savour of life unto life. And who is sufficient for these things? For we are not as many, which corrupt the word of God: but as of sincerity, but as of God, in the sight of God speak we in Christ" (2 Corinthians 2:14–17).

I will endeavor to show that God has great delight in the atonement of Christ. Whether people are saved or lost, a full revelation of Christ must do great good, and will produce great and obvious changes in the character of those who hear. God will be as truly honored in the damnation of those who reject salvation, as in the salvation of those who truly receive Christ.

God has great delight in the atonement of Christ.

This is evident from scripture; examine Philippians 2:5–11: "Let this mind be in you, which was also in Christ Jesus: Who, being in the form of God, thought it not robbery to be equal with God: but made himself of no reputation, and took upon Him the form of a servant, and was made in the likeness of men: and being found in fashion as a man, he humbled himself, and became obedient unto death, even the death of the cross. Wherefore God also hath highly exalted Him, and given Him a name which is above every name: that at the name of Jesus every knee should bow, of things in heaven, and things in earth, and things under the earth; and that every tongue should confess that Jesus Christ is Lord, to the glory of God the Father." From this passage it appears that God was highly pleased with the atonement of Christ Jesus, on account of which "He highly exalted Him, or gave Him a name above every name."

Consider also Isaiah 53:10–12: "Yet it pleased the Lord to bruise him; he hath put him to grief: when thou shalt make his soul an offering for sin, he shall see his seed, he shall prolong his days, and the pleasure of the Lord shall prosper in his hand. He shall see of the travail of his soul, and shall be satisfied: by his knowledge shall my righteous servant justify many; for he shall bear their iniquities. Therefore will I divide him a portion with the great, and he shall divide the spoil with the strong; because He hath poured out his soul unto death: and He was numbered with the transgressors; and He bare the sin of many, and made intercession for the transgressors." Here also God is represented as being so pleased with the atonement of Christ as to give Him a great reward for His labor of love.

God has great delight in the atonement of Christ because He sincerely desires the salvation of people. He knew it was impossible to save them upon the principles of His government without an atonement. And His delight in the atonement of Christ as the means of their salvation is equal to His desire for their salvation.

The self-denial of Christ must have been greatly pleasing to His Father. What virtuous father would not consider himself as greatly honored by the exhibition of such a spirit as Christ manifested in dying for His enemies? When God saw

His Son willing to leave the realms of glory, to take upon Him the form of a servant, to deny himself even unto death for the sake of making the salvation of His enemies possible, this must have been infinitely pleasing to a God of love.

His whole life and death under the circumstances in which He lived and died must have been infinitely pleasing to God. Consider His life, under circumstances of such trial, so spotless, so meek, so just like God, such an exhibition and illustration of what God is, His death, so submissive, so Godlike, it must have come up before His Father "as an odor of a sweet smell."

The bearing of the atonement upon the world must have given it great value in the sight of God. But I shall enlarge upon this thought under the next heading.

A full revelation of Christ must do great good, whether people are saved or lost.

This must be true, because it fully reveals and demonstrates the infinitely great love of God for the world. If the province of an earthly monarch were betrayed into rebellion by slander and the insinuation of selfishness in the government, would it not be highly honorable to the sovereign, instead of sending forth his armies to crush and slay them, to send forth his son to expostulate, instruct, and insure them of the disinterested love and good will of the government toward them? Now suppose that this son, associated with the father in the government, should go forth, not at the head of an army, but alone, unarmed, unattended, unprotected, should go from town to town, on foot, taking unwearied pains to instruct them, healing their diseases, spending whole nights in prayer for them, and when persecuted in one town should go to another. Suppose that he should continue this course of teaching, of expostulation, and of prayer, and when at last they rose to murder him, should meekly allow himself to be crucified, rather than injure a hair of anyone's head. Would not such a demonstration as this, of the love and devotion of the government to its people, greatly confound its enemies and greatly honor the sovereign? Who cannot see that it certainly would?

A full presentation of the atonement must do great good whether sinners are saved or lost, because it fully contradicts the slander by which mankind was drawn off from their allegiance to God. The serpent instigated our first parents to rebellion by insinuating that God was selfish in prohibiting their eating of a certain tree. It was necessary, therefore, that this slander should be thoroughly repelled and refuted. The infinitely great and disinterested love of God exhibited in the atonement is the most impressive refutation of it.

The full portrayal of the atonement of Christ must benefit many, because it fully justifies God as having acted solely under the influence of perfect love, and condemns sin as forever unreasonable, inexcusable, and abominable.

Such an exhibition of the atonement must do great good because it demonstrates God's great willingness and desire to save His enemies, whether they will be saved or not. It rolls the responsibility of their salvation or damnation upon themselves. It proves that while they have forfeited their lives, God has no desire to take this forfeiture at their hands. It proves that while they deserve to die, He has no pleasure in their death.

The atonement manifests the great value of their happiness in His estimation, and His great reluctance to punish them. His love for them was so great as to give His only begotten Son to die for them and He accounted the death, even of His own Son, as a lesser evil than their destruction, notwithstanding they so infinitely deserved to be destroyed.

A full presentation of the atonement of Christ does great good, whether sinners are saved or lost, because it must establish forever the confidence of all holy beings in God. Except for the atonement, the universe might have been open to the surmise that there was something lacking in the dealings of God with the inhabitants of this world. But the unconditional love of God, manifested in the atonement, must forever put His character entirely and eternally beyond all suspicion.

Exposure of the lost to the atonement of Christ must do

great good, whether they are saved or not, because it reveals to sinners, to the whole world, and to the universe, the sincerity of God, by exhibiting the fullness of the provisions of grace. It demonstrates that the provisions are ample, that there is love and grace enough in God's heart, and ample fullness in the provisions of the gospel for the salvation of every sinner. This stops every mouth, and leaves the damnation of every sinner to be wholly chargeable upon himself.

Such an exhibition of Christ must produce great and manifest changes in the character of those who hear.

This must be the case because they cannot but receive or reject it. If they receive it, it will of course make them holy, fill them with love for God and others, and mold their whole character into the image of Christ. If they reject it, it must greatly confirm their selfishness and depravity, greatly harden their hearts, and place them in an attitude of greater and more daring, odious and shameless rebellion than before.

Such an exhibition of God as is made in the atonement must of necessity either subdue or greatly aggravate the spirit of rebellion and hostility to His government. It is impossible that it should not be so. If this exhibition of love does not subdue a sinner, it is because of his unbelief. And he cannot disbelieve the infinite and unselfish love of God in view of the atonement without virtually charging God with the most abominable hypocrisy and with everything that is hateful.

His soul must take this attitude, or it must consent to the truth as it is revealed in the atonement. Now the consent of the heart to this truth must fill the soul with love and the life with holy conformity to His law. But the rebellion of the heart against this truth must greatly deepen and strengthen and forever confirm the reign of sin in the heart and life.

Such a great change of feeling as must necessarily result from an understanding of the atonement of Christ must be manifest in the temper and life. With but little knowledge of God, sinners may proceed in the indulgence of their lusts without being sensible of any direct hostility to God. But when He reveals His love to them in the atonement, they must necessarily either take strong ground against Him, or repent, abandon their sin, and give up their whole being to His influence. This knowledge must necessarily produce an immense change in the temper of their mind toward God. Before, they knew and perhaps thought but little of Him. But after understanding the atonement, they cannot but know and think much of Him. And the attitude of their minds must be that of ferocious resistance and rebellion, or of gentle and Christ-like obedience. Such a change of the temper as this must and will manifest itself in some way in their life.

When Christ is fully preached, people must be fully subdued, or confirmed in sin. Note that I say, *fully* preached. It is amazing to see how many sinners have sat under what is supposed to be the gospel, and yet have little more knowledge of Christ than a heathen. They have never as yet conceived the idea of the love of God, as exhibited in the atonement, and remain as quiet, and as self-complacent as a Pharisee, without ever being stirred up on the one hand to opposition, or on the other to submission. But when Christ is so revealed as to force light upon the sinner's conscience, and compel him fully to understand the doctrine of atonement, the office, relation to God, and love of Christ, as a sin-pardoning, sin-subduing Savior, the soul must soon be conquered or confirmed in sin.

God will be as truly honored in the damnation of those who reject Christ, as in the salvation of those who receive Christ.

Christ will be truly honored, because it will be known He did all that the nature of the case required to save those who are lost. When they had ruined their lives, He didn't give up on them. When they infinitely deserved damnation, God pitied and spared, and sent His Son to die for them. They are the ones who refused salvation through the gospel. They would neither obey the law, nor repent and be forgiven—

nothing that infinite love could do for them could persuade them to accept salvation.

His sending them to hell after manifesting so great a desire to save them will most impressively demonstrate and illustrate His holiness and justice. So great was His pity and love for them that He would sooner die himself, in their behalf, than send them to hell. Yet, so great is His holiness and justice, that when they refuse salvation upon the only principles that can reconcile justice and mercy, He does not hesitate to send them to the depths of hell. If an earthly sovereign should order his own children to execution for rebellion against the laws, would not this be an impressive exhibition of his regard to public order, and of attachment to the principles of his government? What an amazing reluctance did God manifest in the atonement to sending sinners to hell. And after such an exhibition of bleeding mercy, if He is obliged to send them to hell, how infinitely honorable to Him will be such a display of His holiness and justice.

The damnation of the finally unrepentant will greatly increase public confidence in God. What a glorious magistrate is this, how infinitely desirous to avoid public execution, and yet so attached to the principles of His government, so in love with order, so high and holy is His regard to the public interests as to sentence His own children to an eternal hell, if they persist in rebellion. And those very children for whom His love is so great as to have laid down His own life for them! What must the universe think of a sovereign that could do this! What an infinitely holy and glorious king is this! And how must such an exhibition as this establish forever the confidence of all holy beings in Him and His government.

The damnation of the wicked, as rejecters of the gospel, will attribute to the law of God great power. The death of Christ has magnified the law and made it honorable, has manifested God's great regard for it and demonstrated that sooner than repeal it or allow it to be trampled under foot, He would give His own Son to die, that a way might be opened for setting aside its penalty in consistency with the honor of its precept. The damnation of the wicked will greatly strengthen the power of His law by showing that so high is God's regard for it that when so costly an expedient for setting aside its penalty had failed to subdue the sinner, He would execute its penalty upon him in spite of the fact that His love and compassion for him is infinitely great.

This subject sets in a strong light the error of those who represent God the Father as being angry with Christ, and as seeking His vengeance upon Him, and all such like representations. Rather, God says, "This is my beloved Son in whom I am well pleased." Instead of God being angry with Christ, He was infinitely pleased with Him for undertaking the work of redemption.

From this subject, we see that sinners cannot rob God of His glory. Sinner, you need not suppose that the atonement will be lost to the universe, although you reject it. It may be worse than lost to you. But to God and to the universe, it will not be lost. Not one drop of the blood of Christ was shed in vain. And whether you accept the atonement or not, God's government shall receive the full benefit of Christ's atonement.

We see the mistake of those who hold to a limited atonement, and allege as a main argument in its support that if Christ died for all people, then He died in vain for those who are finally lost, and that such a provision is null and void. Now this stems from the supposition that the revelation of God in the atonement is to have no bearing upon His character and government in any other world than this. Rather, it is based on such a narrow view of the moral ramifications of the atonement, that it is not perceived that in the estimation of those who are saved, a real provision for those who reject salvation, would be infinitely honorable to God.

We see from this that the value of the atonement is not at all to be estimated by the number saved. If not one sinner were saved, if all mankind persisted in rejecting it, the exhibition of that love which is made in the atonement would be infinitely important to the universe in confirming His holiness and strengthening the power of His government.

We see also that, to the government of God, the usefulness of ministers is not at all to be estimated by the number of persons saved under their ministry. Look at the text: the Apostle says, "For we are unto God a sweet savor of Christ in them that are saved, and in them that perish. To the one we are the savor of life unto life, and to the other the savor of death unto death."

If ministers fully exhibit Christ, God is as truly honored when people reject, and are damned, as when they believe, and are saved. They cannot but be useful to the universe in proportion to their faithfulness. Their usefulness respects God and His government. To the sinner they may be "a savor of death unto death." But unto God they are "a sweet savor of Christ not only in them that are saved, but in them that perish." They hold forth the love of God in Christ. In this God is glorified, and Christ is preached, in which they "do rejoice and will rejoice," and in which all holy beings will rejoice, sinner, whether you are saved or lost.

The opposition excited by preaching Christ will as truly glorify God as the holiness produced by it. I say nothing of the degree to which the one or the other will glorify God. But that in both God will be truly glorified. If the preaching of Christ produces holiness, God will be glorified by it. If sinners rise up and oppose, it will only further illustrate the nature of sin, and the character of sinners, and more impressively illustrate His justice in their damnation.

Neither God nor ministers aim at the damnation of sinners, nor rejoice in their destruction when they are sent to hell. But they do rejoice in the triumph of justice in that infinitely glorious exhibition of God's character which is made in their destruction.

The more earnestly God and ministers desire and labor for the salvation of sinners, the more their final damnation, if they are lost, will glorify God. If God the Father, Son, and Holy Ghost; if ministers and Christians all labor earnestly and honestly, and with all long suffering for the salvation of sinners, and they will not be saved, then sinner, remember when you go weeping and wailing along down the sides of the pit, God's justice will be the more glorious by how much the greater pains have been taken to save you.

To promote the salvation of people and to honor God in their damnation, ministers must have strong and manifest sympathy with God. The more strongly they sympathize with God the more fully will they exhibit His great desire to save people. And the more fully they exhibit God the more thoroughly do they strip the sinner of all excuses and show that his damnation is imperiously demanded by the principles of eternal righteousness.

Ministers glorify God in proportion as they preach or exhibit the whole gospel. If they pour out before the sinner the whole heart of Christ, if they exhibit Him in all His love, relations and offices, if they unveil the fullness of His compassion and grace, they are removing the sinner infinitely far from all excuses, and rendering his damnation at every step a more illustrious and impressive exhibition of the holiness of God.

Opposition to the preaching of Christ is to be expected, though certainly not desired. Though the damnation of the sinner will still glorify God, yet how much the more his salvation. In addition to which his salvation is a great good in itself, and that which God and all the heavenly hosts greatly desire.

But if sinners will oppose and reject the gospel, ministers should not be discouraged by it and feel as if they are doing no good. My brother, if you are really preaching Christ, glorifying Him and revealing His character in your pulpit, in your life, and in all your ways, you are certainly doing a great good in this world before God and man. If every sinner in your congregation were to go to hell, you should not be discouraged, my brother. "Hold up the hands that hang down, and strengthen the feeble knees."

But do you say that your compassion is great for them,

and you cannot bear to be a savor of death unto death to them? How shall you meet them in the Judgment and see them sent to hell; your neighbors, the people of your prayers and many tears, the souls for whom your heart has groaned, and agonized, and bled? My brother, remember this, God pities them more than you do. Christ's heart has bled for them more than yours. They are the people for whom He has not only prayed and wept, but for whom He has actually died. How shall He meet them in the Judgment, and weep over them as He did over Jerusalem, and say, "O sinners, sinners how often would I have gathered you as a hen gathereth her brood under her wings, and ye would not. O that thou hadst known the things that belong to thy peace. But now are they hidden from thine eyes . . . How shall I give thee up? How shall I deliver thee? How shall I make thee as Admah? How shall I set thee as Zeboim? My heart is turned within me, my repentings are kindled together."

O my brother, lift up your thoughts to the compassionate but infinite holiness and firmness of Christ. He knew how some sinners would treat His atonement; nevertheless, He died for them. He knew that He would be to some a savor of death unto death; yet He knew that He should greatly glorify God by dying for them and offering them mercy. And now my brother, be willing to show forth in your body the dying of the Lord Jesus. Be willing to make up in your self-denying labors and sufferings for their salvation the sufferings of Christ that remain, that through you, God may be glorified, that you may be "unto God a sweet savor of Christ both in them that are saved and in them that perish." Here we have the true ground of consolation, when we see people hardening under our ministry. If in revivals of religion we estimate the good that is really done by the number of conversions only, we overlook one important item: the amount of glory that shall redound to God. The truth is, in revivals of religion, ministers are not only a sweet savor of Christ in those who are converted, but also in those who are hardened.

To the one class they are "a savor of life unto life, and

to the other of death unto death." In both these classes God is greatly glorified. Everyone may know and is bound to know what effect the gospel is producing on himself, and whether it is to him the "savor of life unto life or of death unto death." We should observe its effect upon our families, and carefully watch its influence upon the minds of all around us, and extend ourselves with all our strength to make it the savor of life unto life. But if through the perverseness of the sinner's heart, he will make it the savor of death unto death, let us rejoice not in his hardness nor in his destruction, but in the fact that the holiness and justice of God will be the more gloriously illustrated in his damnation.

And now sinner where are you? Have you ever realized the circumstances of awful solemnity and responsibility in which God has placed you? Do you know what you are doing? Do you understand the requirements which the gospel ministry extends to you? Do you not tremble when you see your minister, and know that God has unalterably ordained that he shall be unto you the "savor of life unto life, or of death unto death?" Do you know that he is the messenger of God to your poor soul, and that you can no more prevent his being to you a savor of life or death, than you can prevent your own existence? Sinner, Christ has not died in vain. Ministers do not preach in vain. Christians do not pray in vain. The Holy Spirit does not strive in vain. Heaven from above does not call in vain. Hell from beneath does not warn in vain.

God's mercies are not in vain. The gifts of His providence are not in vain. His judgments and rebukes are not in vain. All these influences are acting upon you. They *will* act, they *must* act. They *must* be to you the "savor of life unto life, or of death unto death." How infinitely solemn and significant are your circumstances. How dreadful your responsibility! How short your life! How near your death! Are you prepared for solemn judgment? Sinner will you go down instantly on your knees, and offer up your whole being to God, "before wrath come upon you to the uttermost?"

6

CHRISTIANS, THE LIGHT OF THE WORLD

"Ye are the light of the world. A city that is set on a hill cannot be hid. Neither do men light a candle, and put it under a bushel, but on a candlestick; and it giveth light unto all that are in the house. Let your light so shine before men, that they may see your good works, and glorify your Father which is in heaven" (Matthew 5:14–16).

I shall show that the world is in great spiritual darkness; that Christians are to enlighten the world, and how they are to do it. And finally, I shall show that if the world is not enlightened, it is the fault of Christians.

The world is in great spiritual darkness.

Unrepentant sinners are universally ignorant of the true God. Yet, many of them may have a correct theory in some respects. But after all they do not know God. To know God and Jesus Christ is to have eternal life. And while in their sins, they have no correct apprehension of the true God. They are in great darkness in respect to the spirituality of His law. If they understood the holiness of His law, they would understand something of God's character and of their own.

The truth is, they have no correct comprehension of the true spirit and meaning of God's law. Here let me say that when we speak of the spirituality of God's law, there are many who seem to turn away from us as if we were speaking very mystically. "What?" they say, "Law is law. We can understand what God's law says as well as you can, and do understand it as well as you do. Why should you mystify it, and speak of its spirituality as if it had some occult meaning which none but the initiated can understand?" To this I reply: (1) Surely, law is law. (2) Every law has its *letter* and its *spirit*.

The general statement of its propositions in words is its letter. The true intent and meaning of it, in its real application to every state of facts, is its spirit. Now, the world is in total darkness with respect to the true meaning of the law of God. For example, the first commandment is, "Thou shalt have no other gods before me." Now this command has both its letter and its spirit. And so has every commandment of God. Its *letter* prohibits all idolatrous worship. Its spirit requires supreme, disinterested, universal, perpetual love to God, with every holy affection carried out in every holy action.

As a further illustration, take the commandment, "Thou shalt not steal." The letter of this commandment prohibits the secret taking of another's property and using it as if it were our own, without intention of returning it. But the *spirit* of this commandment forbids all covetousness and requires us to love our neighbor as ourselves. It prohibits our using our neighbor's goods, selfishly, whether with or without his consent.

It prohibits every form of fraud, speculation, and taking any advantage in business that is inconsistent with the royal rule, "Thou shalt love thy neighbor as thyself." Now, don't you know that unconverted sinners are in the dark with regard to the spirituality of these and every other command of God? What horrible conviction and consternation would fill the world if sinners but thoroughly understood the spirituality of God's law!

Sinners are ignorant of themselves. They know very little of their own constitution, and in most cases still less of their character. This ignorance of their own character is a natural consequence of their ignorance of the law of God. Being ignorant of the true intent and meaning of the standard with which they are to compare themselves, they are, of course, utterly mistaken in regard to their true character. Judging of themselves only in the light of the letter, and overlooking the breadth of the spirit of the law, they, of course, form an estimate of their character altogether different from the true one.

Sinners are altogether ignorant of their true condition. Being ignorant of the spirituality of the law, they know neither the number nor the exceeding demerit of their sins. Sinners know not their own helplessness nor do they understand the remedy which God has provided for healing their souls. They neither care for, nor know but little about the remedy because they are ignorant of their disease. Sinners are ignorant of what is really good for them, and what will in the highest manner promote their own well being, both in time and eternity. Consequently, sinners are pursuing exactly the course that must eventually and necessarily result in their everlasting destruction from the presence of the Lord and the glory of His power.

Christians are to enlighten the world.

If you are a Christian, you must enlighten the world, because you have the true light. Christians know God. They understand the spirituality of His law. They know the character of man. They know his guilt, helplessness, necessity and true condition. They have seen their own ignorance, and know that the world is in darkness and lieth in wickedness. They have the most certain knowledge of this, and the best of all knowledge, that of their own experience. They also know the remedy for sinners. They have been enlightened by the true light—true Christians have all been taught of God. They know God through Jesus Christ, whom to know is life eternal, and are conscious of that life abiding in them. They can truly say, from their own consciousness, "Whereas I was blind, now I see." They are, therefore, the persons, and the *only* persons who are capable of enlightening the world.

It is in vain for unconverted philosophers or statesmen, or any unconverted person whatever to talk of enlightening the world. The light that is in them is a great darkness. And when they talk of enlightening the world, they don't know what they are talking about or what they are affirming. They speak randomly, deceiving their followers. They are blind leaders of the blind, and they all stumble on together upon the dark mountains till teachers and disciples fall into the pit of destruction together.

The world must be enlightened through human instrumentality. Constituted as we are, truth must address us through the medium of the senses. Consequently God found it necessary to unite himself with human nature in order to enlighten us. Taking to himself human nature, He lived, conversed, ate, drank, and held conversation with men through the medium of His human nature. And this possessed their minds of the true idea of who and what He is. He exhibited in His own life, and in all His deportment, the spirit of His own law. By His teachings, but more especially by His life, He called the attention of men away from the *letter* to the *spirit* of His law. When He gave them precepts, He gave them illustrations of their meaning in His own example, and thus possessed their minds of the nature of true religion, and what it was to love their neighbor as themselves. No one has had the true light but those who have received it through the instrumentality of the saints of God.

From the earliest period of man's existence, God has caused the light to shine upon the world through human beings. Sometimes He has had but few representatives on earth. And gross darkness has covered the whole face of the earth, except here and there a little spot has been lighted up by some pulpit or saint of God. Noah was a light to the former world in its worst state. Daniel was a light in the idolatrous court of Nebuchadnezzar. Prophets and holy men have been scattered up and down on the earth enough to preserve the true knowledge of God. The Lord Jesus Christ, first in His forerunner John, next in His own person, afterward in His apostles, and now in all His saints, is enlightening the world. His people are now the medium through which He reveals himself to mankind. His spirit dwells in them "working in them to will and to do of His good pleasure." They are His disciples who teach His doctrines, exhibit His spirit, and thus at once rebuke and enlighten the darkness of the world.

How Christians can enlighten the world.

What constitutes the Christian's light and renders him a light to others? I answer that it is not simply his creed or profession. Nor is it his profession and creed together. It is not his sanctimonious appearance on the Sabbath or his sitting at the communion table. Nor does his light consist in all these together. But, his light consists in his temper, in his spirit, and in his good works in strict regard to the universal law of love. In short, he lives as Christ lived on the earth. His life is a commentary on the law of God. He is constantly illustrating by his own temper, spirit and life, the true intent and meaning of the law of God.

The Christian enlightens the world by his practical and firm opposition to all that is unholy or injurious to the souls or bodies of men, and in the manifestation of his undying attachment to whatever is holy, lovely and of good report. Christians will not enlighten the world by conforming to the world's disposition, views or practices, nor by any direct or indirect condoning of their sins, worldly mindedness, or other manifestation of darkness.

Christians should not make any compromise of principle. Nor should they conciliate the world's favor by keeping out of view the points of difference between themselves and sinners. Some professors of religion seem disposed to avoid all controversy with impenitent men, to lessen as far as possible the differences of opinion, views, and practices between themselves and sinners. They seem to think that the true way to enlighten them is by falling in with them as far as possible and by conforming in a great measure to their customs, views, business practices, and almost everything else. Now, this is far from the true philosophy of enlightening the world. It is as if you attempted to clear the eyesight of your neighbor by putting out your own eyes. It is like trying to pull the mote out of your neighbor's eye, not by plucking the beam out of your own eye, but by filling your own eye both with beams and motes. If you wish to convince a man that he is in the dark, you must hold up your own light in contrast with his darkness. If he can see your light it will reveal his own darkness.

Christians can never enlighten the world by implying that they lay but little stress on the points of difference between them and sinners. It is in vain to attempt to enlighten the world by any course of conduct that is calculated to make the impression that the real difference between saints and sinners lies merely or mostly in opinion. Christians must not demonstrate that their opinions have very little to do with practice.

Christians *can* enlighten the world by holding up the light of their own example on all subjects in strong and constant contrast with the example of the ungodly. They can enlighten the world by a patient and firm perseverance in well doing, in spite of all the opposition of earth and hell. To what a wonderful extent did the apostles and first Christians succeed in enlightening the world! This was a thing of course. Their lives were a perpetual light, dissipating the moral darkness around them. They did not hold forth a flickering, wavering or uncertain light. It was clear, steady, pure, and had well nigh banished darkness from the earth. In the text Christ says, "Let your light so shine before men that they may see your good works and glorify your Father which is in heaven."

"So shine."

How? By consistently exhibiting your good works in contrast with their evil works.

Christians can enlighten the world by doing the following: (1) By consistently exhibiting self-denial in contrast with the sinner's self-indulgence. (2) By exhibiting our heavenly mindedness in contrast with their worldly mindedness. (3) By showing that our conversation is in heaven in contrast with their conversation which is of the earth. (4) By showing that our treasure is in heaven in contrast with theirs which is on the earth. (5) By showing our conformity to correct principles in contrast with their disregard of the same. (6) By showing our conformity to the laws of our being in contrast with their shameless violations of them. (7) By manifesting our faith in Christ in contrast with their unbelief. (8) By manifesting our sweet submission to all the providential dealings of God in contrast with their restlessness and rebellion against His providence. (9) By holding up on every subject and in every way, both by precept and example, the light of truth in opposition to their darkness. In these and in similar ways can Christians enlighten the world. However, by blinding the light, by making any compromise, by frittering away the points of difference, by moving one hairsbreadth aside from the love of truth for the sake of conciliating their favor, the Christian cannot and never will enlighten the world.

If the world is not enlightened, it is the fault of Christians.

Christians have the means of enlightening the world. They have the gospel and the means of spreading it throughout the world. They have the true light in their own hearts, and the means of exhibiting it to all mankind. They have abundant opportunities to enlighten the world. God has stationed them in different parts of the world for this very purpose. He has commanded them to go, and given them the means of going and holding up their light in every dark corner of the world. When the early Christians clung together in Jerusalem, He scattered them in all countries by the force of a persecution. And they "went every where preaching the gospel." And being thus scattered, they learned the true philosophy of enlightening and converting the world.

The world is looking to Christians and expecting them to enlighten them. The eyes of ungodly people are turned to the Church, marking their example, taking knowledge of their lives, spirit and ways. Wherever among professing Christians there is a true Christian, his light is seen expressly to rebuke the darkness around him.

If the world is not enlightened, it is the fault of Christians, because, if the truth is properly and fully exhibited, it will dispel their darkness. The human mind is so constituted that truth "commends itself to every man's conscience in the sight of God." There is no mistake about this. The human mind is true to its own laws. And when truth is clearly, strongly, and constantly exhibited, it will and must rebuke the darkness of any human mind.

The principal business which Christians have in this world is to enlighten the world. When Christ returned to heaven, He left Christians as His representatives to carry out the revelation of God and shine as His lights in the world. If He should take all Christians immediately from the world, it would leave it in impenetrable and hopeless darkness, in spite of all that has been done to enlighten it. There must be illuminating illustrations of religious truth.

People's minds are so dark, they are prone to view religious truth in the abstract, as a matter of opinion. Without living illustrations, truth seldom, if ever, gains possession of their minds.

Christians are at fault then, if the world is not enlightened, because they have access to any degree of spiritual illumination which they need to do the job. Christ has promised you the Holy Spirit, and has told you that God "is more willing to give it than earthly parents are to give good gifts to their children." Every needed aid is abundantly guaranteed by the same promise of God to Christians.

And in full view of these exceeding great and precious promises Christ has said to them, "Ye are the light of the world." And now "let your light so shine before men that they, seeing your *good works*, (not merely hearing your good doctrines, but seeing your *good works*), may glorify your Father who is in heaven." Nothing can prevent your enlightening the world but a refusal on your part to perform good works.

If you perform good works people will see them. If they see them they will be constrained to glorify your Father which is in heaven. If then people are not enlightened, it is because you do not perform good works. In other words, it is because you are not Christians. Observe Christ does not say, "ye ought to be the light of the world."

Christ says, "Ye *are* the light of the world." As the word of Christ is true, real Christians are the light of the world. And this is a matter of fact. True Christians have the Spirit of Christ, for the possession of this Spirit is what constitutes them Christians. The Spirit of Christ will always manifest itself in performing the works of Christ. If therefore people do not see your good works, and glorify your Father which is in heaven, it is only because you have the form, and not the spirit of Christianity. And "if the light that is in you be darkness, how great is that darkness." Let me conclude by remarking about how much evil is done by modifying or keeping hidden the great and numerous points of difference between Christianity and the spirit of the world. We cannot show ungodly people the necessity of a great and radical change in themselves by conforming in any measure our lives and tempers to theirs.

It is only by strong and constant contrast that the conviction of the necessity of a radical change in themselves is to be forced home upon them. The more striking and constant this contrast, the better. The more universal and perfect this contrast is, the more sudden and irresistible will be their conviction of the necessity of a great and radical change in themselves. We see from this subject how utterly unwise it is to conceal the true light on any great subject of reform, whenever a favorable opportunity should present itself to hold it up. Some ministers and professing Christians seem to be always waiting to have people find out the truth themselves, and for such a public sentiment to be formed as will anticipate and render it popular to hold up any heretofore unpopular or offensive doctrine.

They do not seem inclined to go ahead and rebuke the darkness of the public mind by holding up the true light.

Perhaps they dread the loss of their own popularity, and as they say, fear to injure their usefulness by calling things by their right names, by declaring their own experience of the power of the gospel of the blessed God, by at once preaching and bringing out the whole truth before the world. In order to render themselves popular with all parties, they will hold forth certain unpopular truths in such a way that those who truly promote them will perceive that they believe them. But they will do so with such implied conditions and exceptions, that no one else will suspect them of believing or teaching any such thing. If the whole Church or a local congregation were but to get right without their instrumentality, if a public sentiment should be formed that would invite their coming out in plain language, they would then become bold champions for the truth. But they are waiting for the churches to learn the truth before they declare it to them. And when it becomes popular to tell the whole truth, they will be the first to tell it.

The same is true of multitudes of professing Christians in respect to their lives. For their worldly mindedness, and for all forms and degrees of conformity to the world, they plead the force of public sentiment, that it will not do to differ from everybody else, and that the law of expediency demands of them a good degree of conformity to the world in order to secure an influence over them. But is this the way to enlighten the world? Instead of setting yourself to correct public opinion, do you allow yourself to become the mere creature of it? Instead of opposing what is wrong in the views and practices of mankind on every subject, do you fall in with them, and thus strengthen their bands and confirm them in their darkness, expecting that by and by public sentiment will change so that you can do your duty without losing your influence, so that you can declare what God has done for your soul, relate your experience of the power of His grace, and hold up your light in the midst of the acclamations of the crowd? What a delusive dream is this!

Christians should remember that silence on any great subject of moral reform, that hiding their light either in precept or example when a suitable opportunity occurs for exhibiting it implies either that they do not believe it, or that it is with them a mere matter of opinion, and that they lay little or no practical stress upon it. Or else it implies that they are ashamed of it.

How cruel to let people remain in darkness through a fear of losing our own popularity. On what multitude of subjects are people injuring both their bodies and their souls for lack of correct information. And how shameful and cruel it is for those who have the true light to hide it.

We see from this subject the importance of believers in the doctrine of entire sanctification in this life holding up this infinitely important doctrine, both by precept and example, whenever they have the opportunity. They should be "living epistles known and read of all men."

Unless Christians hold up the true light in contrast with the world's darkness, they are the greatest curses that are in the world. They are like a false light that decoys the unwary mariners upon the rocks and quicksand. The world knows that you profess Christ, that you are set as a moral lighthouse. They therefore think it safe to steer in the direction in which your light indicates they should go. If therefore the light that is in you be darkness, what a curse are you to your family, your neighborhood, and the world around you. They will look at you. They mark your words. They ponder well your temper, spirit and life. They feel themselves safe in copying your example, in drinking in of your spirit, and in steering their course to eternity by your light. And what a cruel monster you are if you mislead them.

What do you say of pirates who erect a false light upon some shoal to decoy the unwary mariners to dash upon it for the sake of plunder? Does not your blood curdle in your veins? Do not cold chills run over you? Does not your soul shudder when you read of the abominable selfishness of those who hold up false lights to mariners at sea, destroying so many lives and property for the sake of gratifying their odious selfishness? But professing Christian, you are the light of the world. Do you hold up a false light in the midst of the world's darkness? And when thousands of sinners are hovering round about upon your coast, benighted and be-stormed and looking to you for light, are you engaged in your selfish projects, exhibiting a carnal, earthly, and devilish spirit, while they are running upon the rocks and quicksand, ruining their souls, and going to hell by scores around you? Hear the wail of that lost soul as it dashes upon the rocks and sinks to hell. It lifts its eyes and cries out, "Oh, I did not dream that evil was near. I had my eye upon that professing Christian. I transacted business upon the same principles upon which I saw he transacted his. I kept my eye upon him and steered my bark by his light. And Oh, unutterable horror, I am in the depths of an eternal hell!"

7

COMMUNION WITH GOD

"The grace of the Lord Jesus Christ, and the love of God, and the communion of the Holy Ghost, be with you all. Amen" (2 Corinthians 13:14).

In discussing this subject, I shall consider the meaning of the term *communion*, what is implied in communion with the Holy Spirit, how we may know whether and when we have communion with God, the value and importance of communion with God, and how to secure and perpetuate it.

The meaning of the term *communion* as used in the Bible.

Communion sometimes means friendly conversation, as in Genesis 18:33: "And the Lord went His way, as soon as He had left *communing* with Abraham." Sometimes it means counsel, advice and instruction. 1 Kings 10:2 reads: "And she came to Jerusalem with a very great train, with camels that bare spices, and very much gold, and precious stones: and when she was come to Solomon, she *communed* with him of all that was in her heart." It is the same term in the original that is rendered *fellowship* in Philippians 2:1: "If there be therefore any consolation in Christ, if any comfort of love, if any *fellowship* of the Spirit, if any bowels and mercies." And John says, "That which we have seen and heard declare we unto you, that ye also may have *fellowship* with us: and truly our fellowship is with the Father, and with His Son Jesus Christ" (1 John 1:3). To *commune* with God, then, is to have *fellowship* with Him, friendly conversation, consultation, advice, and instruction.

What is implied in communion with the Holy Spirit.

To have communion with the Holy Spirit implies that He is a moral agent, and not a moral attribute of God. He is actually and personally present, and indwelling, in the heart of him with whom He communes. He must be actually present with our spirit to render it possible to commune with Him. The communion kept up between the Holy Spirit and all His saints in every part of the world implies both the omnipresence and the omniscience of the Holy Spirit. It implies infinite love and condescension on God's part to allow such as we are to consult and commune with Him, to hold frequent and protracted private interviews with Him, and to commune with Him of all that is in our hearts. This is surely infinitely great condescension.

To commune with the Holy Spirit also implies a disposition in us to consult Him, and commune with Him, in respect to our duty, His will, and the affairs of His kingdom, and it implies a disposition in Him to be consulted by us. It indicates a constant readiness on His part to admit us into His presence, to give us audience, to listen attentively to all that we have to say, and to encourage us to lay open our whole case before Him.

Communion with God implies a sense of our own ignorance and deep dependence upon Him. We seek communion with God in proportion as we are emptied of dependence upon ourselves. A person who is not deeply sensible of his own ignorance will not seek communion with God for the purpose of receiving instruction of Him. A person who is not emptied

of self-dependence will not seek to lay himself down in the
arms of the Savior.

Communion with the Holy Spirit implies that He takes
the deepest interest in us. Surely His interest in us must be
exceedingly great to be willing to hold consultation with us
so often, to commune with us so deeply, to enter so much into
the details of all our affairs and interest himself in our slightest grievances, trials and difficulties. To do this constantly
and without weariness or impatience certainly implies on
His part a most profound interest in us. To be able to commune with God reveals there is a deep sympathy and fellowship between the Holy Spirit and us, so that we feel as He
does and He feels as we do. This implies that we have a
common object in view, that we are influenced by the same
motives, interested in the same objects, employed in the
same labors.

In short, it implies that our fellowship and sympathy
with Him are equal to our communion, for they are in fact
the same thing.

How we may know whether and when we have communion with God.

When we are conscious of being drawn by His silent but
powerful influence, and are very near to Him in prayer, we
know we have communion with Him. Every true Christian
knows what it is to feel a secret moving of heart toward God;
a silent, but deep, powerful meeting, drawing of soul away
from the world, from society, from business, from everything
else, into a most sacred private interview with God.

In such cases the soul seeks to be alone with God. It naturally follows, crying after God, and its desires are like a
liquid stream, flowing and flowing. As he is on his way to
some secluded spot, or upon his knees in his closet, or perhaps
in the night season upon his bed, "his heart and his flesh cry
out for God, for the living God." From the depths of his heart,
his soul cries out, "Father, Father," and repeats and echoes,

over and over, all the dear names and titles of God, and their associations to his mind. His soul seems to be as fluid—flowing, rising, falling into the deep waters of His love.

We have communion with God when we have great freedom and enlargement in prayer. Sometimes the soul feels unutterably burdened with conviction and distress, but has no words. It is bowed down to the earth, but cannot express, nor even think over in any order, its sins, its burdens or its sorrows. It seems to be shut up to God, and yet feels as if it could not approach and fully lay the heart open before Him. But at other times, there is great freedom and enlargement of mind. Our thoughts and words flow like a river. We find not only our desires enlarged, but our views of ourselves and of Him greatly enlarged. We have a kind of supernatural ability to express ourselves in a most emphatic and elevated manner in pleading our cause before Him. There seems to be room enough in the benevolent yearnings of our hearts to embrace the universe. We seem, as it were, to embosom the whole race and bring them before God in earnest longings and with strong cryings and tears that He would have mercy on them. We seem to see everything and feel everything and express everything on an enlarged scale. We enter into such a deep sympathy with God as to feel our whole souls drawn away with benevolent desires. In this state of mind we may rest assured we are in communion with God.

We have communion with God when our necessities are laid open to us. Sometimes we are hard and dark. We know that something must be wrong, but have no clear idea of what it is. I speak now of the case of those who have not yet learned to abide all the while in the light. But those who have made the greatest attainments of any persons in this world, no doubt, often feel their spiritual necessities laid open before them in a most remarkable manner. If not conscious of present or recent sin; yet, they are often made to see how vastly they fall short of what they should have been had they never sinned at all.

How much ignorance, how much weakness, how many

infirmities are upon and about them in consequence of their former sins and habits of selfishness. God often draws us into deep communion with himself and has protracted and close interviews with us, sometimes for hours and even days together, for the purpose of kindly calling our attention to and laying open before us those particulars in the character and infirmities in which we need greater measures of His grace. He makes us to see the depth of our ignorance, how weak we are under temptation, and how certainly we shall be overcome, but for His ever present grace. In this state of mind, we may be sure that we are in communion with God.

When we are able to spread our whole case, and open up the deepest necessities and secrets of our hearts before God, we are in communion with Him. We sometimes feel as if we could go to the very depths of our whole being and bring forth every secret thought, affection, emotion and whatever has been deep and concealed, and spread them out in the light of His countenance.

When we are enabled to bring forth our strong reasons in pleading with God, we are in a state of communion with Him. Sometimes we find ourselves able to plead and reason with God, as a man would plead with his friend, to bring forth our reasons and array our arguments with a strong confidence and almost assurance that they will affect his mind as they do our own. The reasons which we offer to God appear to be weighty and sufficient to our own minds. And we feel a kind of supernatural confidence that they will and must and do influence the mind of God. We press Him with them. As we turn them over and over; lay them out in their connections and bearings and feel as if they could not be resisted. We insist upon their weight and force, and often urge them upon God with a kind of supernatural vehemency of spirit which refuses to be denied.

This was no doubt the state of Jacob's mind when he wrestled all night with God. This state of mind is what is intended by wrestling with God. In this state the soul uses the strongest language, feels the utmost confidence in the ground it takes, takes hold of the very strength of God, and casts its whole being upon Him with the strong reasons which it urges, and upon his immutable faithfulness and promises. But this state of mind is only understood by those who have experienced it. The stranger cannot understand such things as these. If any cold-hearted professing Christian or ungodly sinner could be concealed in some secret place, and witness the secret conversation of such a soul in communion with God; and if he could listen to his language, behold his streaming perspiration, the whole scene would, no doubt, impress him with mingled feelings of wonder and consternation.

When we feel like consulting God on almost everything that interests us and concerns the interests of His kingdom, we are in communion with Him. Christians sometimes feel, and many habitually feel, a disposition to ask God's opinion, consent and advice at every turn. They seem to abide in that state of mind in which Paul was, when he said, "Lord, what wilt thou have me to do?" With others, less advanced in grace, this feeling is not so habitual. Yet all true Christians know what it is to feel their hearts drawn into an attitude of constant consultation with God, a fleeing and running to Him for advice, a breathing out its supplications to Him for counsel, a disposition to consult Him about the minutest things and mention to Him even the most trivial occurrences and circumstances of life. In this state the soul feels like a very little child consulting a most wise and affectionate father.

Whenever we feel disposed to make God a sacred confidant, and disclose to Him all those secret things which we would confide to no other being in the universe, we are in a state of communion. The Christian's soul is sometimes drawn into such a state as to feel an intense longing to treat God as the most sacred and confidential friend, laying open before Him all those secret things about which no other being has any right to know or give an opinion. The Christian's soul is united to God, and sustains a thousand endearing and interesting relations to Him that it sustains to no other being. It is sometimes compared to the married state. But it almost infinitely exceeds it in the deep and sacred confidence it reposes in God. No conjugal confidence ever began to equal it: the sweet, sacred, deep, profound confidence of the soul in God. No husband ever laid open to his wife, or wife to the husband, the deep springs of action, the most retired and secret workings of the soul as one in communion with God will often do. Oh, the unspeakable confidence which the soul feels when it discloses to Him the deepest, darkest, profoundest necessities of the whole being.

When the Scriptures are opened to our understandings and made to take hold upon our hearts, we are in communion with God. A soul not in communion with God may be interested in the Bible as a history; but its more spiritual parts are like a sealed or an uninteresting book. The mind's eye will wander over chapter after chapter, browse through its sacred pages amidst all the glories it reveals, without being struck, fixed, and held as by enchantment in view of its glorious developments. But when in communion with God, every sentence bears the impress of God. It is full of meaning, full of light and love. It discloses the very secrets of the heart of God and lays his very being bare to our inspection. The soul pauses at every sentence, and wonders, admires and adores. It looks into the deep profound. The spiritual world is open to its view. It seems, as with a telescope, to have bidden eternity into his presence. And the whole spiritual world seems to be so uncovered before him that he is almost in the state in which Paul was, not able to tell whether he is in the body or out of the body. It is easy for a mind in this state to conceive what Paul meant when he said, "I knew a man fourteen years ago, whether in the body or out of the body, I cannot tell; God knoweth; I knew such a one caught up into the third heavens, and heard unspeakable words, which it is not lawful for a man to utter." The fact is, his mind was so entirely absorbed with the objects presented to his spiritual eye; his attention was so entirely engrossed with them, as to be unconscious of the presence of any objects of sense. And he could not afterward tell whether he was in the body or out of the body.

It is related of Xavier that his communion with God was so intense that when he retired for secret devotion, he was obliged to leave word with his servant to call him at a certain hour. Sometimes his servant would go, after he had remained for hours in secret communion with God, and find him upon his knees, the Bible open before him with his eyes fixed, and lost in deep, secret communion with God, so that his servant would be obliged to shake him before his attention could be so drawn off from spiritual objects as to be conscious that he was still a resident of earth. I have myself known instances in which persons were very much in this state of mind.

Now there are many degrees of this kind of communion with God, when the Scriptures are so opened up to the mind, so understood, and its truths so apprehended and appearing to the soul so glorious and ravishing, as to swallow up in a greater or lesser degree the thoughts, attention and whole being.

When we are made deeply sensible of our character, past and present, we are in communion with God. Sometimes Christ has fellowship with the soul, and calls its attention to a great many things that make it vastly ashamed of itself. The whole soul is filled with shame, confusion and blushing. The Holy Spirit gently but thoroughly opens up to the mind, the past and the present, and lifts up the veil of oblivion, quickens the memory, and as it were causes our whole character to stand out before our mind's eye like a hideous and unseemly ghost. The soul in this state seeks to find the very lowest place in the whole universe. It cries out, from its deepest foundations, "Oh, to get infinitely low before God." Sometimes persons in this state of shame, self-abasement and unutterable self-abhorrence, seem not at all to be aware that this is communion with God. Being in the habit of considering communion with God to consist altogether in those joys which the saints sometimes experience, they do not realize that these deeply self-abasing thoughts and views are only the result of a close and searching interview with God. In this state of mind, they sometimes feel as if God had forsaken them, and can see it to be so infinitely reasonable that He should, as not to be aware that they are now, perhaps, more thoroughly in the light and really in a state of more deep and thorough communion with God than perhaps they have been at any other time.

We are in communion with God when we have great confidence in Christ. The mind is sometimes filled with adoring views of the fullness there is in Christ, such as Wisdom, Righteousness, Sanctification and Redemption. It oftentimes, when drawn into this form of communion with the Holy Spirit whose business it is to take the things of Christ and show them to us, sees in Him such infinite fullness and security, such a world of promises, so vast in their meaning, so true, so infinitely certain in their fulfillment, that they are all yea and amen in Christ Jesus. The soul feels at such times that it is indeed complete in Him; that He is a perfect Righteousness, a perfect Sanctification, a perfect Redemption; that His grace and fullness are large enough to swallow up all thought, all finite conception; that the sins of all mankind might be merged in the ocean of His grace; that all the temptations, wants and woes of man might all be swallowed up in the boundless ocean of His love and grace, and would all be only as a pebble in the midst of the great Pacific Ocean. At such times, the mind can see that in Christ dwells the fullness of the Godhead. It feels itself set upon an everlasting rock, in a large place, and its goings established. It feels such vast repose in Christ that "as the mountains are round about Jerusalem, so is the Lord Jesus Christ round about them that fear Him."

When we are spiritually minded, we are in communion with God. All those states of mind of which I have spoken are forms of spiritual-mindedness.

But here I mean a state of spiritual-mindedness in general, upon every subject; a habitual minding of spiritual things in opposition to minding earthly things. In this state, a man, while he lives in the flesh, is, after all, much more conversant with the spiritual and heavenly world than with the men and things of this world. He indeed walks upon the earth; however, his conversation is in heaven. He is surrounded with sensible objects, but he is so little interested in them that he scarcely heeds them. His soul has come into the light, as God is in the light. It walks and lives in light. It is bathed in the very sunlight of heaven. Spiritual objects are stronger and more impressive realities than sensible objects. Such a soul, and such a one only, can understand the full import of Paul's language when he said, "I am crucified with Christ: nevertheless I live; yet not I, but Christ liveth in me: and the life that I now live in the flesh I live by the faith of the Son of God, who loved me and gave himself for me" (Galatians 2:20). The soul in this state is in a marvelous attitude. The soul is in the body, and of course able to converse with sensible objects, and yet, so in the Spirit as to be able to hold sweet, intimate, and continual communion with the Holy Spirit. It can repose its head as upon the very bosom of Christ while its feet are standing upon the earth.

When we have victory over our spiritual enemies, we have communion with the Holy Spirit. The soul in communion with God can easily bid Satan to depart, and he flees. Its faith seems to have the strength of omnipotence. It seems to vanquish all its spiritual foes with the utmost ease. The mind in this state rises above spiritual enemies and the power of temptation. The waves of temptation that would at another time overwhelm it seem to break harmless at its feet. It stands upon a rock above them. Temptation cannot reach it, but spends its impotent strength in beating against the everlasting rock on which it stands. It feels that Christ fights all its battles for it.

It has only to hide in Him, as in the cleft of a great rock, and Christ says to the winds and waves of temptation, "Peace, be still," and there is a great calm.

Now, beloved, do you know anything about these states

of mind? If you do, you know what it is to have fellowship with the Father and the Son through the Holy Spirit.

There is one more form of communion which I will mention, and that is when the soul is swallowed up, and all its will and desire lost and merged in the will of God. In this state of mind, the soul feels as if it had not and could not have any will of its own, any wish or desire that anything in the universe should be in any respect different from what God would have it. It feels that it has and can have no interest of its own, aside from the interest and will of God. His interest, His kingdom, and His will are its all. If in any case it is uncertain what is the will of God, it feels as if it could make no other petition in respect to that event than "Thy will be done." It feels such an attachment to the will of God, such confidence in it, as infinitely right and benevolent, as to feel as if it never could have a wish, desire, or thought, inconsistent with the will of God. It feels as if the least rising of opposition against the will of God, the least lack of most entire resignation, were more to be dreaded and more terrible than hell itself.

I must continue this discourse in the next sermon.

8

COMMUNION WITH GOD/PART 2

"The grace of the Lord Jesus Christ, and the love of God, and the communion of the Holy Ghost be with you all. Amen" (2 Corinthians 13:14).

In pursuing this subject, I shall continue according to my plan in chapter 7.

The value and importance of communion with God.

Communion with God is just as important as a true knowledge of God. No one really and truly knows anything of God, unless God reveals himself personally to that soul. I do not mean by this that He must make to him a revelation not made in the Bible; but God will cause him to know and comprehend the true meaning of the Scriptures by the Holy Spirit. "No man can say that Jesus is the Christ, save by the Holy Ghost." No one understands anything more than the letter of the Bible, unless he has direct and personal communion with God. The Bible is not a revelation to anyone without this personal and direct opening up of its truths to the soul; it is only "the letter that killeth." Bible truth is to the unenlightened no revelation of God; it is but blindness, darkness and mystery. This fact does not seem to be under-

117

stood even by many in the Church: that direct communion
with God will result in the Holy Spirit's explaining, as it
were, His own word, and making the Bible a direct and personal revelation to the believer.

Again, without this revelation of the word, no one has a
true knowledge of God. Scripture itself teaches that "to know
God and Jesus Christ is eternal life." But do all who have
the Bible know God and Jesus Christ? Do all who read and
even study the Bible know Jesus Christ, and have eternal
life? Surely not. None know God and Christ in such a sense
as to have eternal life unless He is directly and personally
revealed to them through the Word by the Holy Spirit. What
vast and ruinous error exists in the Church concerning this
subject. Communion with God is also just as important as a
true knowledge of ourselves. No one has a thorough knowledge of himself beyond what has been revealed to him
through his communion with God. The human heart is naturally such a deep pit of darkness that we absolutely need a
revelation of ourselves as much as we need a revelation of
God. God is the only being in the universe who knows us.

We are naturally lost, bewildered and in almost total ignorance of our own true character. In our long and frequent
communion with God, He takes occasion, as it were, in our
protracted conversations to spread out before us our own history, to reveal us to ourselves, to command up from the deep
oblivion of our own forgetfulness past occurrences in our
lives. In His light and in the light of His law alone, do we
ever come to a right knowledge of ourselves. Oh, how infinitely important is that communion with God that reveals
man to himself.

Communion with God is as important as our need to be
saved. No one is truly saved without that communion with
God of which I have been speaking, for the simple reason
that he cannot be saved without the knowledge of God and
of himself. It is also absolutely indispensable to his being
sanctified and prepared for heaven.

Even our usefulness to others is not more important than

our communion with God. In fact, it is the lack of it that is at the root of the inefficiency of the Christian ministry. Many ministers lack deep fellowship with God, walking in the light of the Scriptures, conversation with God on a level which unites him with His will and purpose for the Church, and unction from the Holy Spirit in their preaching.

Oh, what is a minister that does not keep up communion with God? As well might an alien, an enemy, or a rebel be employed as an ambassador, as a minister hold office and attempt to deal with sinners in the name of God without communion with Him. My ministerial brethren, will you allow me to ask you, in the kindness, sincerity and sobriety of my soul, whether you understand in your own experience what I have been talking about? Do you know, dearly beloved, in your own experience, what this communion with God is? Do you live in His light? Do you walk with God? Is your lifestyle in heaven? Do you feel as if your soul were wafted on an ocean of His love by the trade winds of His eternal Spirit? Do your people, when you enter the pulpit, see your soul stand out before them bathed in the sunlight of heaven? Do your prayers, preaching and all your ways impress them with the conviction that you are a spiritually minded man, that you are risen with Christ? Do they know that your heart is not set upon things on earth, but upon those things where Christ sits at the right hand of God?

My brother, my beloved brother, do you preach the spirit or the letter of the gospel? Are you a minister of the New or of the Old Testament? Be not offended, but let me be honest with you in order to help you. Do you want to be useful to your fellowmen? Would you glorify God in all your ways? Does your fruit abound to the glory of God? Are you instrumental in watering their souls with the water of eternal life? Do you feed them with the bread of heaven? What is the state of the church to which you minister? What is the standard of their spirituality? Especially, how is it with those with whom you associate most, and over whom you have the most influence? Do you feed them with the "sincere milk of the word?"

If, by your daily experience, you know what that communion with God is, of which I have been speaking, I might venture to answer these questions for you; but if you do not, you are but a "blind leader of the blind." Be not displeased with this. I speak it in love, and because I deeply feel it. And if you do not know it to be true, the more deeply do I pity you and the church to which you minister: and the more emphatically do I implore you to seek this communion with God. Communion with God is as important as it is so we will not ruin the souls of those around us.

A professing Christian who does not have habitual communion with God is one of the greatest curses to the world. This is because the eyes of the world and of the Church are upon him. By his profession he is publicly set forth as an example and a light to the world. He is professedly the representative of Christ. He is to be regarded as a living illustration of the truth, nature and importance of religion. He is a "living epistle, known and read of all men." But if he has no communion with God, there is nothing in him that resembles God. He becomes earthly, sensual, worldly; the very reverse of what he professes to be. His profession of religion mixed with the spirit of the world makes him one of the greatest stumbling blocks and curses that can afflict the world.

If this is true of any professor of religion, what must be true of a minister of Christ who does not hold habitual communion with God? I do not hesitate to say that he is vastly worse than no minister at all.

The people would be almost better off without any pastor, than to have one who holds little or no communion with God from day to day. The fact is, communion with God is the secret of all piety. Communion with God is absolutely indispensable to the usefulness of ministers and private Christians, and without which they will certainly do almost more hurt than good in the world. Communion with God is important in preventing perpetual dishonor to God. No one can honor God in his walk and conversation without keeping up habitual communion with Him. His life will be a perfect libel upon the character of God, a misrepresentation of God and of Christianity, just that which is most likely to increase and perpetuate the prejudices of the world against God.

Communion with God is important in giving us peace of mind. Nothing so recommends the gospel to mankind as the exhibition of that great peace of mind which they have who love the law of God. To our own happiness, to our own usefulness, to the honor of God, to the interests of the Church and the world around us, our own peace of mind is of vast importance. That we should be able to pass through the storms and trials that keep the world in great fermentation and distress, in calmness and unbroken peace, is a most desirable and infinitely important thing. But this cannot be done without communion with God. When storms arise, the soul must be in such a state as to take refuge in the very bosom of God from where it can look out upon the warring elements with the deepest composure of mind. God's heart is always calm. It is a great and infinite ocean of eternal love and peace. It is infinitely serene, calm and pure; never disturbed by any event, not thrown into a state of upheaval by any or by all the occurrences of the universe.

Now nothing can calm our own minds amidst the shocks, vicissitudes and trials of life, except continual communion with the infinitely calm and peaceful mind of God. Oh, when the soul has been disquieted by the occurrences of life and takes a deep plunge into the ocean of eternal love, when it steals away from all human eyes and holds a protracted and soul-calming interview with God, how peacefully does it look about upon those occurrences that are throwing the world into confusion and lament.

Communion with God is vitally important if we are to have any grace or faith at all. No one, no matter what his pretense or profession, has one particle of Christian faith in exercise any further than he lives in communion with God.

Christ says, "I am the vine, and ye are the branches."

Now communion with God is just as indispensable to the life of religion in the soul as the sap of the vine is to the life of the branches.

How to secure and perpetuate communion with God.

Communion with God must be sought. God will be inquired of by the house of Israel to do those things for them which they need. The soul must desire communion with God.

It must seek it. It must prize it above all else. If you desire communion with God, do not neglect Him and go into communion with other gods. Allow no idol to have any place in your heart. Allow nothing of any name or nature to draw your heart away from communion with Him. See that your heart does not in the least degree become divided between God and some other object of affection. Be sure not to neglect His counsels, when He condescends to commune with you and give you advice.

Whatever He shows to be your duty, do it at all cost. Do not in any case or for any consideration confer with flesh and blood. Spare not a right hand, or a right eye; but whenever He shows you the path of duty, let it be the fixed purpose of your heart to enter upon it at once without discussion or hesitation, even if you face injury or death at every hand.

Avoid everything which you would avoid if He were visibly present with you. Consider how you would act and what you would do if Christ stood physically before you, or God were pouring the blaze of His searching eye upon all your ways. If you mean to keep up communion with God, be as holy in heart, life and conversation as you would be were Christ your visible and constant companion. Engage in nothing that shall in any way interrupt your communion with Him. Engage in no such kinds of business or adopt business principles which are inconsistent with living and walking with God. Read no such books, have no such companions, spend no time in such a way as is inconsistent with a state of entire consecration to God. Keep your whole heart open to Him. Let the door of your heart, as it were, stand open, and your heart lie spread out continually before God.

Habitually and daily lay the secrets of your whole heart before Him. Cultivate this, and rest not short of keeping your whole mind and heart transparent before God, nothing covered or in the least degree veiled or concealed from the inspection of His eye. I do not speak thus because I suppose anything can be concealed from God; but because it is one thing for God to see through your whole being, whether you will or not, and quite another for you to come voluntarily and allow Him access to your whole heart.

Give yourself wholly up to His guidance. Let it be the fixed purpose of your heart to spare no idol, indulge no sin, to do or say anything, think or be anything than that which is in exact accordance with His guidance and instruction. Have no more desire or thought of varying a hairsbreadth from His instruction than you would of taking your own life, or leaping into hell.

Do not allow your communion with God to be interrupted but for one hour. Let the medium between your heart and God be so clear that the least change of atmosphere shall at once alarm your soul. Whatever you are engaged in, wherever you are, let your very first business be to inquire what it is that is causing the Sun of Righteousness to shine more dimly upon your soul. Do not be satisfied until you ascertain and remove the cause. At all cost, you must set your heart upon keeping in the pathway of the just, that shineth more and more unto the perfect day. Better, vastly better for you, to sacrifice any worldly good and make any earthly sacrifice, than to have your fellowship with God at all interrupted. It is better far to live in a dungeon, in communion with God, than to sit upon a throne in an earthly frame of mind.

Expect in your communion with God adequate guidance and grace. "His grace is sufficient for thee." If it was sufficient for Paul, under the circumstances in which he was, it is sufficient for every saint. Do not be afraid then to ask and expect great things. The greater things the better. "Open your mouth wide," He says, "and I will fill it. Call unto me and I will answer thee, and show thee great and mighty things which thou knowest not." And remember that He is able to do "exceeding abundantly above all that we ask or think." He has told you that "it is more blessed to give than to receive." If, therefore, you limit His giving by your unbelief, you grieve His heart. You cannot do Him a greater injury than by your unbelief to prevent His bestowing upon you the blessings He so greatly desires to give.

Show Him that nothing is more valuable to you than communion with Him. Let Him see that you will deny your appetites, your fleshly desires, and whatever would in the least degree divert you from Him. Do not surround yourself with idols, nor with such creature comforts as will show Him that you do not believe Him to be a sufficient portion. He calls you His bride. Let your soul be satisfied with His love and wander not at all after other lovers. Let Him see that you consider Him an all-sufficient and infinitely satisfying portion, and that you desire no other.

Form no unnecessary attachments to any being or thing on earth. Guard your heart as you would guard the apple of your eye. "Keep thy heart with all diligence, for out of it are the issues of life." Remember that the Lord your God is a jealous God; you cannot have communion with Him and communion with the world at the same time.

Aim just as much at being *wholly* consecrated to Him as you aim at being religious at all. Have no thought and make no calculation at all inconsistent with this. Form no plans, entertain no desires and engage in nothing whatever that shall be in the least degree inconsistent with your being as holy as He is holy. Be sure, as far as possible, to avoid temptation.

It would seem as if the great mass of professing Christians are either perfectly blind in regard to exposing themselves to temptation, or that they think themselves able to overcome in their own strength. I have often been struck and even shocked at the state of mind in which those persons are who deny the doctrine of entire sanctification or entire consecration to God in this life. It is evident that they expect to continue to sin as much as they expect to live, that they make all their calculations accordingly, that they do not so much as mean to live in a state of entire consecration to God—not even for a single day.

A minister friend said in my hearing that on being requested by another minister to engage in a certain business which he feared would be a great temptation to him, he declined upon the ground that he feared that in doing so he should sin. His brother replied, "And what of that? We are sinning all the time. If we sin, we simply must repent, you know." Now I cannot tell you how many instances I have seen similar to this among professing Christians. It puts in a most striking and abhorrent light the belief that Christians are not to expect to be entirely sanctified until death.

Now, let me tell you before God and the Lord Jesus Christ, that which, if you are a Christian, you know to be true: you cannot live in communion with God unless you give yourself up to Him in a state of entire consecration. Whenever you are overcome by sin, your communion is interrupted, of course. Unless you really intend and expect to be wholly and perpetually consecrated to His service, keeping up communion with God is impossible.

Communion with God cannot be perpetuated without watching unto prayer, and praying in the Holy Spirit. "Pray without ceasing, with all prayer and supplication in the Spirit; watching thereunto with all perseverance and supplication for all saints." It is a vain dream to expect to keep up communion with God in the neglect of frequent and protracted seasons of secret prayer. When a certain man was asked whether he prayed in secret, he replied, "When my friends are absent I write to them, but when they are with me I have no need to write." But I would ask such a one, "When your friends are with you, do you not so much as speak to them?" Communion with God implies what is equivalent to talking with God. And more than this is implied in communion with God. It implies the most intimate and confidential interchange of views and feelings that can be conceived. Let no one dream that his communion with God will continue for any length of time if he neglects to offer much, very much secret prayer.*

How few keep up communion with God! Sinning willfully against the light may cut off communion between your soul and God forever. I have known some lamentable and distressing cases where persons by one willful sin brought themselves into a state of protracted, if not final, despair.

Communion with God is the secret of all ministerial effectiveness. Here let me say that ministers often deceive themselves respecting their effectiveness in the church. Through the instrumentality of faithful, spiritual members of their church, there may be true revival, entirely independent of their own instrumentality. This, I have good reason to know, is often the case, and further that they are often supposed by others to be eminently instrumental in promoting the salvation of souls, when, as a matter of fact, they are an obstacle! It is to be feared that they often think themselves in a good degree effective, because they live so far from God they cannot see that they are in reality doing more harm than good.

In the light of this subject, we can also see the results of ministerial unfruitfulness. Christ says, "Abide in me, and I in you. As the branch cannot bear fruit of itself, except it abide in the vine; no more can ye, except ye abide in me. I am the vine, ye are the branches. He that abideth in me, and I in him, the same bringeth forth much fruit; for without me ye can do nothing. If a man abide not in me, he is cast forth as a branch, and is withered; and men gather them, and cast them into the fire, and they are burned. If ye abide in me, and my words abide in you, ye shall ask what ye will, and it shall be done unto you. Herein is my Father glorified, that

---

*See *Principles of Devotion* for Finney's sermons on prayer and on attaining and maintaining communion with God.

ye bear much fruit; so shall ye be my disciples" (John 15:4–8). In this passage Christ seems expressly to teach that if ministers are unfruitful or if any Christian is unfruitful, it is because, as a matter of fact, he does not abide in Christ. Abiding in Christ is keeping up constant communion with Him. Now as these words of Christ are true, no professing Christian and no minister has a right to say that he abides in Christ, if he does not "bring forth much fruit."*

From this subject we see the importance of students keeping up communion with God during the progress of their education. It is, I believe, one of the greatest and perhaps the most common and damaging error among students to suppose that they can give up in a great measure communion with God while pursuing their college education. They suppose that they shall naturally resume it again when they enter upon the study of theology, or when they shall enter the ministry. Now, beloved young man, let me warn you against this delusion. It can be fatal to your future usefulness. Inquire the world around among all the fruitless ministers of your acquaintance, and you will find almost without exception that this has been the "stone of stumbling" to them. They were pressed in their studies. They gave up communion with God for communion with authors, teachers, and their fellow students. They became earthly, sensual, worldly. The results of their ministry can tell you the consequences of their folly.

The privileges of Christians now are greater than if they enjoyed the personal presence and preaching of Christ. Christian, what would you say if you could have Christ for your pastor? Should you not expect to grow in grace? Would you not expect to live a life of entire consecration to God? Hear what He says: "Nevertheless I tell you the truth; it is expedient for you that I go away: for if I go not away the

---

*See *The Secret of the Abiding Presence*, a devotional book from the writings of Andrew Murray and Brother Lawrence. Published by Bethany House Publishers.

Comforter will not come unto you; but if I depart I will send him unto you ... Howbeit when he, the Spirit of truth, is come, he will guide you into all truth: for He shall not speak of himself; but whatsoever he shall hear, that shall He speak: and he will shew you things to come. He shall glorify me: for he shall receive of mine, and shall shew it unto you. All things that the Father hath are mine: therefore said I, that he shall take of mine, and shall shew it unto you" (John 16:7, 13–15).

Further, "These things have I spoken unto you, being yet present with you. But the Comforter, which is the Holy Ghost, whom the Father will send in my name, he shall teach you all things, and bring all things to remembrance, whatsoever I have said unto you." Here then, we have the express declaration of Christ that the presence of the Holy Spirit which we may always enjoy is of more importance to us than His personal teachings. Christ could not be everywhere in His bodily presence. But the Holy Spirit is everywhere. Christ could only instruct us by His words and example were He personally present with us. But His Spirit can directly approach our minds and put us in possession at once of the whole truth. Christian brother, sister, ministerial brethren, I beseech you, understand your privileges and know that as a matter of fact they are greater, if you will lay hold of them, than if you lived in the same house, ate at the same table, enjoyed the daily conversation and personal preaching of the Lord Jesus Christ himself.

Oh, then keep up constant communion with God. And may the grace of the Lord Jesus Christ and the love of God, and the communion of the Holy Spirit be with you all. Amen.

9

TEMPTATIONS MUST BE PUT AWAY

"And if thy right eye offend thee, pluck it out, and cast it from thee: for it is profitable for thee that one of thy members should perish, and not that thy whole body should be cast into hell. And if thy right hand offend thee, cut it off, and cast it from thee: for it is profitable for thee that one of thy members should perish, and not that thy whole body should be cast into hell" (Matthew 5:29, 30).

In discussing this subject I will show that things which in themselves are lawful and even important may become a cause and source of stumbling to the soul by sinful indulgences. Furthermore, however dear and important they may be, if through abuse they are the cause of our falling into bondage to sin, then they must be put away. I will also show that to continue to allow the temptation in such cases, and expect grace to overcome, is to tempt God. If any form of temptation is allowed to have dominion over us, and we succumb to it without repentance, we are inevitably and forever lost.

To allow anything, however lawful and important, to become a stumbling block in our lives, is plainly implied in the text. It clearly lays down a principle, and a strong case is presented by way of illustration. If thy right hand or thy right eye offend thee; that is, cause thee to offend, then cut off the hand and pluck out the eye. What is more important to us than a right hand or right eye? It is as if the Savior had said, "If these things, which are so important to you, do in fact become a snare and lead you into sin, put them away." It is plainly implied that the most lawful and useful things may become a snare to our souls. Everyone should be aware that his eyes, his ears, his friends, his employments, his possessions, his bodily appetites, and multitudes of other useful things, may by perversion be made a snare to the soul.

However dear and even important they may be, if through abuse they are the cause of our falling into bondage to sin, they must be put away.

Our own good demands it: "For it is profitable for thee that one of thy members should perish and not that thy whole body should be cast into hell." It must be put away, because if we prize it more highly than God, it is our idol and our god. Our god is what we hold in highest regard. If we supremely love God, we would rather part with anything than offend Him. Hence Christ teaches that unless a man hate his father, mother, brother, sister, and even his own life for Christ's sake, he cannot be His disciple. If anything is loved or prized more highly in comparison to God, we have no religion at all. If a person does not dread sin more than he dreads death, he is no disciple of Christ. If there is anything in the world that he loves more than he hates sin, anything whatever that he would rather spare, even though it keep him in bondage to sin, he is not and cannot be a true disciple of Christ.

I speak, of course, of those things that can be put away by us by an act of self-denial on our part. If there is any degree of self-denial which we would not prefer to being bound in sin, then according to the Bible we are not disciples of Christ. Please understand, I am not speaking of some rare and high attainment in piety, but of a normal condition of discipleship. Christ uses the strongest language without seeming to fear being misunderstood. He says, "If any man come to me, and hate not his father, and mother, and wife, and children, and brethren, and sisters, yea, and his own life also, he cannot be my disciple."

To continue to allow temptation in such cases, and expect grace to overcome it, is to tempt God.

Christ taught us to pray that we may not be tempted. Now what is tempting God, if this is not: to pray that we may not be tempted, without using all the means in our power to avoid temptation? Suppose a drunkard should pray against temptation to intemperance, and still keep his cupboard loaded down with all kinds of liquor? I know some say that they have set some tempting object continually before them to show the strength of their resolution to overcome. Whether there is any truth in such reported cases I do not know. But this I *do* know, it is very unwise. It is nothing less than tempting God to allow a temptation, which actually brings us into sin, to continue before us and exert its influence upon us, when it can be simply removed by our own hand. It is tempting God, because grace was never designed to purchase exemption from self-sacrifice and self-denial. Grace will enable us to make right choices, and support us in the hour of unsolicited temptation.

It is enough for the servant to be as his master. Christ, as a man, was obliged to be diligent, to deny himself, and to keep himself clear of those besetments and temptations that would naturally overcome Him.

His Apostles followed in His steps. Paul found it indispensable to keep his body under, to mortify his members which were upon the earth. It is an unalterable law of the kingdom of grace that people must put away those weights and easily besetting sins that hinder and overcome them, or they will never enter into the kingdom of God. Therefore, to

continue in the place of temptation, and expect grace to overcome it is to "turn the grace of God into lasciviousness."

**If any form of temptation is allowed to have dominion
over us, to the point of sin not repented of, we are
inevitably and forever lost.**

We are inevitably lost when we remain in a state of unrepentance. You are an unrepentant sinner if you prefer living in sin to cutting off a right hand or plucking out an eye.
To allow a temptation that prevails over us to continue, when
by an act of self-denial on our part we can put it away, is but
to confirm a state of unrepentance. Every day and hour we
allow ourselves to continue under such an influence, the
bonds of unrepentance are strengthened until we are hope-
lessly delivered up to the dominion of our besetting sins.

To allow this is totally inconsistent with any degree of
holiness—to so supremely love an object so as to refuse to
part with it, even though it leads to sin against God! I say
again, this is not merely a state of defective piety. It must be
a state of no piety at all.

If things of a lawful and important nature in themselves
have become a stumbling block to us and must be put away,
how much more needful that we put away useless and unnecessary things. We can readily see the error of those who
hold on to practices and things which are a cause of stumbling to them on the ground that they are lawful in themselves. What is more lawful or more important than a right
hand or a right eye? Suppose that when Christ delivered the
Sermon on the Mount, of which the text is a part, one of His
hearers had replied, "Surely, this man is mad and hath a
devil. Will He teach us to cut off our right hands and pluck
out our right eyes? Did not God make them for lawful and
useful purposes? Would He have a man maim himself, or
make himself a cripple for life? Is it not lawful for us to enjoy
the good things of providence? This is altogether a legal
spirit, and by no means the doctrine from God."

What reply do you suppose Christ would have made to such an objection as this? And yet how many vehement debates do we hear in which people are pleading for and defending their lusts, indulging their appetites, and ruining their souls on the ground that these things are lawful in themselves? Suppose they are lawful in themselves, and yet it is a fact that you abuse them and allow them to lead you into sin. If they are lawful in themselves, you do not use them lawfully. They have become your masters, instead of your servants; therefore, you must put them away, however lawful they may be in themselves, or you will lose your souls.

We see the mistake and the presumption of those who hold on to things which prove a snare to them on the ground that they are useful things. What is more useful than a right hand or a right eye? Yet Christ says, put them away; for however useful they may be, they will never pay you for the loss of your soul.

We see the folly and madness of those who hold on to their indulgences in things that lead them into sin on the ground that these things are not expressly forbidden in the Word of God. One man can find it no where forbidden in the Scriptures to use ardent spirits, another can find no express passage forbidding the use of wine, and a third can find slavery no where prohibited in the Bible. In short, many seem disposed to indulge themselves in whatever is not expressly forbidden, without at all regarding the actual influence of those things upon them.

How little he cares for sin, or knows of God, who can willingly tolerate that which leads him into sin. What can he know of God? What does he really know of sin? What idea can he have of true Christianity? Surely nothing that is not infinitely distanced from the truth.

From our observations here, it is easy to see that if property becomes a snare it should be put away. If a person's attachment is such that worldly possessions lead him into a state of worldly-mindedness, he should give his property at once to the cause of God and refuse to possess any, even if he becomes as poor as Lazarus. Such a course is altogether indispensable to the salvation of his soul. If his property is a snare, he must put it away, whether it is much or little. Any and every article of property that gets hold of the heart diverts the attention and affections from God, whether it is a dollar or a mine of gold, a horse, a house, a farm, a store, or anything whatever that alienates the soul from God, must be put away, or the soul is lost. Now is this any stronger than the doctrine of the text? Certainly not. If this is extravagant, then Christ is extravagant. If this is not solemn truth, then the text is not true, and Christ was a false witness. I know that such statements are apt to be looked upon as extravagant, but it is no extreme assertion to say that whatever piece of property, or whatever amount of worldly goods seduces the soul away from God, must be given up, once and for all and forever, or the soul is inevitably lost.

What vast madness possesses the souls of those who are endeavoring to get all the worldly goods they can, and even to lay up wealth for their children, when they are knowingly conscious that their worldly possessions are diverting their minds from God and His kingdom? It would seem as if they were enlisted to work out their own damnation with all their might.

If you are inclined to eat too much, you must deny yourself those kinds of foods that lead you into gluttony. Whatever those delicacies are, of which you are so fond, and that overcome you when placed before you, and lead you to transgress the laws of your being, put them entirely away. Do not allow them to find a place upon your table. The exact opposite of this course is generally pursued by mankind. From the general conduct I have observed, it would seem that they fear starvation and that the utmost attention must be paid to preparing tempting dishes, or they would not have sufficient appetite to meet the demands of their bodies.

Now, gluttony is one of the most common sins in the world. It is the testimony of the best judges upon this subject that excessive eating is the most common form of intemperance that prevails among men and women, and is the cause of more disease, especially in this country, than any other form of intemperance. How unwise, how wicked, how utterly tempting God you are, to continue to prepare and set before yourself those elaborate dishes, instead of furnishing your table with those wholesome meals of which you will be likely to eat only a reasonable quantity for your health's sake.

If any article of dress begets pride and vanity, occupies your thoughts, and diverts your mind from God, put it away forever. A woman in one of our large cities, who was justly considered beautiful and had been recently converted, was seen by a friend with her hands full of silk flowers and hairpieces approaching the fire. "What," said the friend, "are you going to do with them?"

"What?" answered the young convert, "I am going to burn them up."

"Oh," said the friend, "Don't burn them up. You can sell them and give the proceeds to some benevolent cause."

"Sell them," said she, "and thus tempt someone else to be as proud and vain of them as I have been? No, I would rather destroy them. They shall no more be a temptation and a snare to any human being." How remarkable to me is the conduct of professing Christians! Knowing their weakness and liability to be overcome by pride, one would suppose that they would avoid even the purchase of articles which might promote pride or vanity, as they would avoid destruction itself. But alas, this is not the case. Under the pretense of consulting good taste, they take the utmost pains, and often spare no expense, in tempting themselves to pride by the purchase of articles that will adorn their persons and show them off to advantage.

Let me just say this then, that whatever of dress, of equipment, furniture, or the like that may produce pride and vanity must be put away, or the soul is lost. Every appetite and passion that builds pride and leads us into sin must be crucified and its dominion entirely destroyed, or the soul is utterly lost. Those who live in self-indulgence, and still think that they know and enjoy Christ, are deceived Antinomians (those who believe faith alone saves, and we have no obligation whatever to obey God's laws).

I have heard some who have professed to come into the liberty of the gospel decry everything that looked like self-denial and mortification of the flesh as legalism and belonging to Judaism, rather than to Christianity. Hence they indulge in the use of wines and strong drinks, and their women indulge in dress and flutter about after the fashions of the world. Because they are now in a *state of liberty*, they spurn and despise a course of temperance, self-denial, cross-bearing, and nonconformity to the world, as altogether a legalistic and self-righteous spirit and course of life. Paul did not do so.

Christ did not do so. Neither does anyone who truly knows Christ. Many seem to think the gospel was designed to purchase indulgence, instead of begetting self-denial. The gospel was obviously designed to enlighten the minds of people in regard to the value of heavenly things, to bring them out from under the dominion of the objects of sense, and engage their thoughts and their hearts in the pursuit and enjoyment of spiritual things; and thus to lead mankind to neglect the glitter and glamor of this world, to forego pampering their appetites, indulging their passions, adorning their bodies, and floating on in the currents of this world. But many seem so entirely to mistake the true spirit and intent of the gospel as to suppose it designed to sanctify conformity to the world instead of entirely delivering the soul from it. This completely distorted understanding of the gospel places many people in a very remarkable state of mind.

I have even heard of a young woman, a professing Christian, who was in the habit of sleeping with a young man as if she had been his wife, and who, before retiring to her bed of iniquity and shameless lust, would kneel down, and very seriously thank God that He allowed her such an indulgence! Now, no doubt she supposed herself to be very thankful, and in a very humble frame of mind.

Although this was an extreme case, yet I have myself seen many things that seemed to involve the same principle, and to be the result of the same utter misunderstanding and perversion of the gospel. These were instances in which persons were manifestly living in self-indulgence, pride, and luxury, and appeared to be very thankful that the gospel had relieved them of the necessity of an opposite course of life, and had actually sanctioned their indulgence in worldly activities.

These same were squandering Christ's money, injuring their health, stupefying their minds, adorning their bodies, and in multitudes of ways making war on both moral and physical law. Yet, having the idea that the gospel sanctioned all this, they were highly pleased with their gospel, their Christ, their salvation: a salvation evidently not *from sin*, but *in sin*, not *from the dominion of the flesh*, but rather one that gives full rein to appetite, lust and vanity. These poor dreamers seem to suppose that under the gospel there is no need of restraining the natural appetites, but that all may be indulged with perfect safety and propriety, if there is only faith in Christ.

Now forever understand that faith in Christ is that which *gives victory over these things*, instead of sanctifying the indulgence of them. What may be expedient for one to possess or enjoy may not be so for another. On account of natural temperament, or the influence of grace, one may have possessions which are not a temptation to draw him away from God which another cannot have. It is never safe for us to possess or indulge in anything because another does so; for it may be that we are not equally able to bear it. Under some circumstances, we may not be able to bear what under other circumstances we could bear without injury.

From these discussions it is easy to see the importance of watchfulness, and of giving the utmost attention to the occasions of our stumbling, whether proximate or remote. When I was a young convert, I was struck with this resolution of Jonathan Edwards: "When I do any conspicuously evil action, I am resolved to trace it back till I come to the original cause, carefully endeavor to do so no more and fight and pray with all my might against the origin of it." No doubt, our eyes should be continually open to all the influences that are acting on us and affecting our moral characters. Every article of dress, everything in our employments, amusements, companions, books, diet, habits, ways, whatever leads us into sin should be put away.

Some indulge temptation and sin until they are so blinded and hardened that they feel no condemnation, and think that all is well. Their consciences have become stupefied and remain indignantly silent. And what they once esteemed to be sin they no longer regard as such. They can now complacently indulge in what would once have made them tremble. And because they *feel* no condemnation, they imagine that they are not condemned. Now it is one thing to have a seared conscience, and to be in that negative state of mind in which there is no felt condemnation, and another thing to have that active, positive, and conscious state of love to God and others in which you have the continual testimony that you please God.

All the promises in regard to support under temptation and deliverance from it are to be understood to be upon the *condition* that we avoid and put away all temptation as far as we possibly can. We often find promises to which no express condition is annexed, but where a condition is either plainly implied or expressed in some other part of the Word of God.

Take the promise in 1 Corinthians 10:13, "There hath no temptation taken you but such as is common to man: but God is faithful, who will not suffer you to be tempted above that ye are able; but will with the temptation also make a way to escape, that ye may be able to bear it." Here is a promise without any condition expressed with regard to deliverance from the power of temptation. But our text is to be regarded as a condition related by Christ to all promises of this nature. And these passages together teach this doctrine:

We need not fall under the power of any temptation that we can avoid or put away from us; when we have gone the full length of sacrificing a right hand or a right eye to be rid of temptation, no unavoidable temptation shall come upon us from which we shall not have grace to escape. This is all that such promises can mean, when viewed in the light of the expressed or implied conditions of the gospel.

If we are not enabled to put away and overcome temptation, it is because we have no savior. The savior's name is JESUS, *because* He saves His people from their sins. If, therefore, you are not enabled to overcome your sins, it must be because you reject the Savior.

How many are engaged in defending their idols and their lusts, rather than in putting them away? If anything is found to be a temptation and a cause of stumbling to us, we should never indulge or defend it because others indulge in the same thing. Perhaps others are able to do it without it being an enormous stumbling block to them. Or if it does overcome and lead them into sin, their destruction is certainly no good reason why we should also be destroyed.

Where a thing may be reasonably suspected as the cause of our falling into sin, it should be put away. Sometimes we are not fully aware of what the particular thing is in our habits which grieves the Spirit of God, and yet have reason to believe that it may be a particular thing. Anything remotely doubtful should never be allowed.

A thing may be overlooked as a cause or occasion of our stumbling, because it is not a proximate but a remote cause. The thing which acted immediately upon us to cause our fall may perhaps be something that we cannot put away. But if we candidly inquired, we might find the more remote occasions, and by removing them continue in a state of liberty.

If a man loves God, he will not and cannot rest until every cause of stumbling is searched out and removed. Can a man love God supremely, and find himself betrayed into sin against Him, and rest without searching out and removing the cause? Certainly not!

Those who secretly dislike the doctrine of sanctification in this life are not Christians. From the manner in which many who profess Christian faith treat this question, it seems obvious that they feel a secret dislike to it. They seem indisposed to understand it. They appear to set themselves on objecting to it and perverting it, rather than honestly and earnestly investigating it with a desire that it might be true. What they say and write often makes the impression upon those who hear and read that there is in the depths of their hearts a spirit of deep opposition to it. Some suppose that this manifested opposition is because it is regarded as error, and that Christians will naturally and rightly evince opposition to error. I should be glad to believe that this opposition is founded in the conviction that this doctrine is false; but there is one circumstance that forbids accounting for this opposition on this principle. When a doctrine is rejected because it is false, the doctrine will be fairly stated and met, and rejected for what it is, and not for what it is not. But, when we see a mind resorting itself to misstatement and misrepresentation in order to evade a doctrine, it is difficult for us to believe that it is rejected because it is believed by the mind to be false.

We can see why so many who admit the truth of the doctrine of entire sanctification in this life do not practically embrace it. They have some idol with which they will not part. Their right hand and their right eye are so dear to them that they will not spare them for the sake of eternal life. This is especially so when the common sentiments of the Church dictate that this is entirely unnecessary. They seem to reason thus: "We are about as good as the average Christian, although to be sure, we are guilty of some sins. The great majority of Christians do not believe that entire sanctification in this life is necessary or even attainable. We can, therefore, satisfy ourselves with but partial sanctification in this life, and still go to heaven. Why then should we give up all our idols, merely for the sake of entire sanctification here, when, in the judgment of the Church, and even the ministers, partial sanctification will do?"

It seems to me that this statement represents the real, though unexpressed, sentiments of many. The truth is, they are unwilling to give up their sins, and they resolve, if possible, to get into heaven without being sanctified. Let us hear again the words of Christ: "If thy right eye offend thee, pluck it out, and cast it from thee: for it is profitable for thee that one of thy members should perish, and not that thy whole body should be cast into hell. And if thy right hand offend thee, cut it off, and cast it from thee: for it is profitable for thee that one of thy members should perish, and not that thy whole body should be cast into hell."

If a temptation is of such a nature that it cannot be utterly put away, we should do everything we can to destroy its influence over us. For example: Our appetites and passions cannot, at our will, be annihilated; but those things that excite them to go beyond the bounds set by God, can be avoided.

How terrible is the delusion of those who expect to be sanctified, or even saved, in the course of life which they are pursuing. It is no wonder that the Church as a whole does not believe in the doctrine of entire sanctification in this life. Too many are satisfied that, with their present habits and indulgences, they cannot be entirely sanctified. And as these habits and indulgences appear to be stereotyped, they reject the doctrine of entire freedom from sin in this life as unreasonable.

Whenever all is done that can be done to avoid temptation and to put away whatever brings us into bondage to sin, we may expect, and are bound to expect, that no temptation shall come upon us from the power of which we are not able to escape. It is then entirely within the reach of every individual to live in a state of entire consecration or sanctification to God.

And now, whatever you do, do quickly. Will you put away now and forever those temptations that overcome you, which can be put away by you? And will you now commit yourself to the keeping and protection of the Lord Jesus Christ to sustain you against the power of those temptations which you cannot avoid? Or will you hold on to your idols but a little longer, until all is lost. Again I say, whatever you do, do quickly. Every moment's delay is grieving the Holy Spirit, and allowing the Enemy a foothold to lead you to destruction.

Professing Christian, and unrepentant sinner, do you realize that while I speak the curtain may be ready to drop, the scene close, and your soul be shut up to the inescapable second death! Do you know "that now of a long time your judgment lingereth not, and your damnation slumbereth not"? The Spirit is grieved, God is provoked, divine forbearance is almost exhausted, and your soul may be nearly forever lost! Again I say, what you do, do quickly.

10

DESIGN OR INTENTION CONSTITUTES CHARACTER

"Give them according to their deeds, and according to the wickedness of their endeavors" (Psalm 28:4).

I understand *endeavors* in this text to mean *design* or *intention*. In discussing this subject, I shall point out the distinction between intention and volition; the distinction between an ultimate or supreme intention and a subordinate intention. I will show that moral character lies mainly in the ultimate or supreme intention, and that the moral character of those actions which are directed by the intention is the same as the ultimate intention. I will also seek to show when the intention is sinful, when it is holy, and that a person's character (as distinguished from the character of any one of his acts) is the same as his supreme and ultimate intention.

The distinction between intention and volition.

Intention is the mind's design, aim or end. It is not the outward object aimed at, but the inward design of the mind to secure a given object. Volition is the action of the will, or those subordinate choices which are produced and directed by the intention. In other words, intention is a state of the will, a permanent disposition distinct from single choices or actions of the will. Volitions are, strictly speaking, the means used by the will, or the efforts which it makes to obtain the object of its design or intention.

The distinction between an ultimate or supreme intention and a subordinate intention.

An ultimate intention is the final end which the mind has in view, and that to which all other ends are subordinate, for they are only a means of fulfilling that intention. For example: A student may work to get money, to purchase books, to obtain an education, to preach the gospel, to convert sinners, to glorify God.

Here are several ends, subordinate to one supreme or ultimate end. The first end which the student has in view is to get money. But this is both an end and a means.

His second end is to purchase books. A third end, the end for which he purchases books, is to obtain an education. But his education is also a means to another end, which is to preach the gospel, and this means to the end of the conversion of sinners. Now, the conversion of sinners is but a means to the end of glorifying God.

Moral character lies mainly in the ultimate or supreme intention of the mind.

Moral character cannot lie in the outward actions. The outward actions of a person, when viewed apart from the intention, have no moral character, any more than the motions of a machine.

Moral character cannot lie in volition, irrespective of intention, for the same volition may be holy or sinful depending on the intention. For example: I may will to use the name of God, and the moral character of this intention must depend upon the design I have in using His holy name. I may will to go to a certain place, or to do a certain thing, but this willing or choosing may be holy or sinful only as my design to go to that place or to do that thing is good or evil.

Everyone's reason dictates that character lies in intention. If a person designs to do us evil, and by chance does us good, we do not thank him for it. And if a person designs to do us good, and without any fault of his own it results in evil, we do not blame him.

The text assumes that the moral character lies in endeavor or intention. Let the case of the student, already referred to, serve as an illustration. The student works to get money. Now it is easy to see that this labor is holy or sinful according to the use which he intends to make of his money. But when we learn that he intends to purchase books with his money, we cannot yet decide upon the moral character of what he is doing. Hence, we inquire what books he intends to purchase and what he intends to do with them. We learn that he wants to obtain an education; but here we are as much at a loss as ever to know what the moral character of his conduct is. We must inquire why he obtains an education. Then we learn that it is to preach the gospel. This looks well so far; but as yet we cannot decide upon the moral character of his conduct. He may intend to preach the gospel to promote his own interest, to gratify his ambition, or with some other sinister design. We must, therefore, pursue our inquiry and know *why* he intends to preach the gospel. He replies that it is to convert sinners. But this does not decide his moral character. Why does he wish to convert sinners? Is it that he may be thought highly of and called a great and useful man, and thus promote his own reputation? We must, then, push our inquiry home and ask *why* he wishes to convert sinners. We are told that it is because he supremely loves God and dearly loves the souls of men.

We learn he desires to promote God's glory and their happiness as things good in themselves, that but for this ultimate supreme end, he would not work to get money to buy books, etc. He is conscious that the ultimate intention, that at which he aims, which is the mainspring and cause of all his choices, and that to which all these other ends are subordinate, is the glory of God and the interests of His kingdom. Here, and not until we arrive here, have we any light in respect to the moral character of his present employment, laboring to get money.

The moral character of those choices and outward actions which are directed by the intention is the same as the ultimate intention.

But for the intention, choices and outward actions would have no moral character at all. The moral character must be decided by the ultimate intention.

We see the student vigorously at work, and know that volition is the cause of all his outward actions.

But the moral character of what he is doing cannot be in these volitions themselves, when viewed separately from the intention, in obedience to which they are exercised. We next see the student purchasing his books; and next, poring over his studies; and again, preaching the gospel. In all these instances, we see a busy will (volition) continually at work. But not one of these choices (volitions), when viewed separately from the intention, would have moral character any more than the choices of a brute. Nor does the moral character lie in any of the subordinate ends. To get money, to purchase books, to obtain an education, to preach the gospel—none of these have any moral character when viewed apart from the ultimate intention of the mind in doing these things. Reason and common sense affirm this.

When the intention is sinful.

When the *intention* is to do *wrong*, although the thing intended may not be in itself wrong, it is sinful. If it is thought to be wrong, and intended as wrong, it is wrong.

When the intention is to do a thing known to be wrong, *not because it is wrong*, but in spite of its being wrong, it is sinful.

Multitudes of human actions come under this category; vastly more, no doubt, than under the first. It is believed that people seldom do wrong for the sake of the wrong; but knowing it to be so, do it in spite of the knowledge, and for some other reason. It is sinful when the intention is to do or not do something, regardless of, and without inquiring into, the moral character of that act or omission. And, of course, when the intention has no respect to the will of God, it is sinful.

When the intention is selfish, it is sinful. Whenever the ultimate end is to secure our own good, this is a state of selfishness. This is wrong, because our own is not the highest good, nor that at which we ought ultimately and supremely to aim. God's glory and the interests of His kingdom are of infinitely more value than our own individual happiness. Whenever our ultimate intention is to secure our own happiness, our whole character and conduct is sinful, whatever means we may employ. We may attend to all religious duties with the greatest zeal, give all our goods to feed the poor, our bodies to be burned, but if we are not motivated by supreme love to God, if our ultimate intention is not to glorify Him, the foundation of our character is utterly wrong.

When the intention is holy.

The intention is holy when and only when it is the ultimate aim, object, or intention of the mind to glorify God and promote the good of the universe. If we design to glorify God as the means of promoting our own happiness, this is selfishness. To glorify and please God must be a thing intended and sought for its own sake and on its own account. Now when this is the supreme and ultimate end at which we aim, the character is holy. In other words, none but a disinterestedly benevolent intention is holy.

If you inquire whether my designing or intending and laboring to promote the glory of God will not result in my own happiness, and may not therefore be regarded as the most remote or ultimate end at which I aim, I answer: (1) To supremely aim at and labor for the promotion of God's glory will doubtless promote my own happiness, (2) but my own happiness in this case depends upon the disinterestedness of my intention of laboring to promote the glory of God.

If, in laboring to promote the glory of God, my ultimate end is my own happiness, I cannot in this way be happy any more than I could be happy in praying, if I should pray, not because of communion with God, but to promote my own happiness. I cannot be happy unless I do that which my whole nature approves. My whole moral being decides that God's glory and interests are supremely important in themselves, and that I should seek to promote them for their own sake and on their own account. In no possible way, therefore, can I be happy unless I act in conformity with this stern and uncompromising dictate of my nature. My happiness, therefore, will result or not result from my intending and laboring to glorify God in due proportion to the disinterestedness of my intentions and labor.

I repeat it, therefore, that although a person's happiness is a consequence of his intending and laboring to glorify God; yet, the intention terminates not at all upon his own happiness as an ultimate end of pursuit, but upon the glory of God and the interests of His kingdom as something infinitely important in itself.

A person's character, as distinguished from the character of any one of his acts, is the same as his supreme and ultimate intention.

We have seen that the character of our acts is of the same character as the ultimate end. A person's character is made up of his ultimate or chief end. Thus, we speak of an avaricious man, an ambitious man, a disinterested man, meaning by such expressions to distinguish the character of the man from the character of any one of his acts. The ultimate end which a person has in view in his conduct may not always be that which occupies his thoughts, and his conduct may be sinful or holy without the ultimate intention being, at the time, the subject of consciousness or even thought.

For example, the student's thoughts may be, for the time being, wholly upon his labor or his books; and yet he may be influenced by the ultimate end he has in view, whether it be ambition or disinterested love to God, without being at all conscious at the time of being influenced by any other than the immediate end before him. But although the immediate object before him is the subject of his thoughts, still his labor or his study is as holy or sinful as his ultimate intention is.

There can be but two classes of people in respect to moral character. There is but one right, ultimate end or intention, which is the glory of God and the interests of His kingdom. This ought to be the ultimate intention of every moral being in the universe. Every other ultimate end or intention is entirely wrong. So that there cannot by any possibility be more than two classes of moral beings with respect to moral character.

From these observations, it is easy to see that unregenerate sinners are, without exception, entirely depraved. We have seen that a sinner's character is as his ultimate intention is. Every unregenerate sinner has a selfish ultimate or supreme intention, and is therefore in a state of total depravity.

From this subject we can see what regeneration is: it consists in the change of the supreme or ultimate intention of the mind.

We can see that two people may act precisely alike, be engaged in the same transactions, and in every respect be outwardly exactly alike, and yet possess moral characters precisely opposite. Nay, they may be both outwardly and inwardly, with the exception of their ultimate intention, exactly alike, and yet possess opposite characters.

They may both will to pray, to go to meetings, to perform every Christian duty. They may will, do, and be exactly alike in every other respect; yet, if their ultimate object or intention is not the same, their moral characters are in the sight of God totally unalike. An action may be morally right, because the intention is so, and yet there may be a sinful ignorance connected with it. A person may make a mistake in the use of means to glorify God. If he honestly intended to glorify God, the action itself is not sinful. Yet, if he was culpably negligent in the use of the means of information, and has used improper means through his ignorance, his ignorance is a sin.

From this subject we can see what we are to understand by the sin of ignorance. The ignorance itself is a sin when the means of information are neglected. If I act wholly from right intentions, that act cannot be in itself sinful; yet, if I am mistaken through ignorance, the ignorance itself may be sinful. Now, some may object that Paul blamed himself for doing what he verily thought he ought to do: "many things contrary to the name of Jesus of Nazareth." It is true that in this case Paul was to blame for doing what he truly thought he ought to do, because he was an unrepentant sinner at the time, and his ultimate intention was not to glorify God; but he thought he ought to do it in obedience to the superstitious and persecuting notions of the Jews. If he had been a converted man at the time, and had his heart set upon glorifying God, he could not have thought as he did, that he "ought to do many things contrary to the name of Jesus of Nazareth." Therefore, even though he thought he ought to do it, his conduct was sinful, because the ultimate design or end of doing it was not to glorify God but to gratify his Jewish prejudices.

Do you see the real distinction between true saints and hypocrites? It does not lie in the fact that they pursue opposite courses of life, but in that they pursue substantially the same courses of life with opposite ultimate intentions. The true Christian's ultimate intention is to glorify God; the hypocrite's intention is his own happiness.

It is easy to see the great danger of delusion, because the

ultimate intention of the mind is so often and so easily over-looked. Here, for example, are two students, just commencing a course of study. Now how many subordinate ends must they pursue, and how remote, so to speak, is the ultimate end at which they aim. They both labor hard, exercise economy, study diligently, and may preach zealously, and be equally useful; and yet their moral characters all along will be entirely opposite. Their thoughts may be taken up so much with the different subordinate ends of pursuit that they may easily overlook and keep out of view the ultimate end or mainspring of all their actions. But herein lies the moral character of all their conduct. And if they are ignorant or mistaken in respect to this, they may, at any period of their lives, drop into eternity with a false hope, but in a state of such deep delirium as to cry out, "Lord, Lord, open unto us. Have we not prophesied in thy name, and in thy name cast out devils, and in thy name done many wonderful works? And then will I profess unto you, I never knew you." We can also learn from this study that the sins of true Christians are not continual and habitual. In other words, they consist in wrong choices rather than in ultimate intentions.

I have said, in a former part of this discourse, that the moral character of those volitions and actions which are caused and directed by an ultimate intention is the same as the ultimate intention. This implies, as I intended it should, that some actions and volitions are not in obedience to an ultimate intention, but in opposition to it, and are caused by the desire of some present gratification. In other words, they may not be in accordance with, but in opposition to, the supreme and ultimate intention of the mind. The moral character of these acts must be determined by the particular design or intention that gave them birth.

A man, for example, may set out to go on a foreign mission with the ultimate intention of glorifying God. Yet, under the force of strong temptation, he may be driven off his course and either commit a single act or a series of acts not in obedience to his ultimate intention or in accordance with it. Nor yet are these acts performed with the ultimate intention of abandoning his missionary enterprise. These acts are not performed in obedience to any ultimate intention, either to glorify God, or to promote his own ultimate interests. But, if I may so speak, they fall out and leave a chasm in his usual course of conduct through the force of temptation without any change of his ultimate design. Their cause is that, for the time being and under the circumstances, the temptation has more power over his single choices than his ultimate intention has. This is indeed a deep mystery, but so it is, however its philosophy is to be explained. I repeat it, then, that the sins of true Christians, while they are voluntary, are in opposition to their supreme intention and are not continuing or habitual.

We see why God does not and cannot deal with people in this present world according to their true character. Every man knows, in his own experience, that he is not dealt with precisely according to his character in this life. It would create vast confusion if God dealt with people according to their ultimate intentions, as they appear to Him.

It is said that "the ploughing of the wicked is sin." Now upon what ground is it sin? The willful choices that regulate the muscles to hold the plough are not sinful. It must be, therefore, that his ploughing is sin, simply because his ultimate intention is selfish. If God punished people in this life according to their ultimate intention, it would require the confidence of angels for one to believe that He was right, and not to stumble at His conduct. One man would be punished for ploughing, and another for praying, and another for preaching, and others for multitudes of things, so far as human observation goes, that are good and praiseworthy. While, on the other hand, many actions would be rewarded, which, so far as human observation goes, would be pronounced sinful. It must, therefore, be true that God does not and cannot deal with people *in this world* according to their real character without perplexing and perhaps ruining the universe.

Do you see from this explanation the necessity of a General Judgment, when God shall disclose the real character of all mankind, to the whole universe, and deal with everyone according as his work shall be? People will be rewarded according to their ultimate intention, whether they have been able to carry it out or not. "Give them," says the Psalmist, "according to their endeavors." This is the language of inspiration.

Here is one man, designed to be a missionary, to save souls, and glorify God. But his health, in the providence of God, has prevented it. Be of good cheer, my brother. God will carry on His work without you, and reward you according to your intentions. Here is another man, who has devised and intended to execute many generous and wonderful things for the Church, but his expectations have been thwarted, and he has been unable to succeed according to his endeavors. Well done, good and faithful brother; you have done well in that it was in your heart to glorify God. You shall be rewarded according to all that was in your heart.

We can see what permanent sanctification is, and when saints are permanently sanctified. They are permanently sanctified when they arrive at that state in which they are not drawn aside in heart and in life to will or to do what is inconsistent with the ultimate intention of glorifying God.

How many professing to be Christians will go down to hell with a lie in their hearts! It is plain to see the secret of the self-righteousness of sinners. They do not judge themselves by their ultimate intention, wherein their moral character lies, but by the subordinate ends at which they aim. If a sinner ploughs, he thinks, surely, there is no harm in this; but on the other hand, takes credit for it, as being in accordance with his duty. He supports his family, goes to meetings, does a thousand things which professing Christians do. He supposes these things to be commendable and virtuous in themselves, irrespective of the ultimate design which lies at their foundation and is the cause of them. In this consists his sad and ruinous mistake.

A man may do wrong, without intending to do wrong. Indeed, it is not common for men to aim at the wrong they do, and do things because they are wrong. A man sins unless he desires to do right, to act in accordance with his duty.

And now, beloved, when tried by this standard is MENE, MENE TEKEL (weighed in the balances and found wanting) written upon your Christian character? Will you honestly go down upon your knees before God, and spread your whole heart out before Him? Will you honestly look into the foundation of your conduct and inquire what is your ultimate and supreme intention? And will you remember that according to your intention God will deal with you in the solemn Judgment?

11

CONFESSION OF FAULTS

"Confess your faults one to another, and pray one for another, that ye may be healed" (James 5:16).

In this discussion I shall show: what is intended by faults in this text, to whom this passage requires confession to be made, the design and use of confessing faults one to another, and that we are under special obligation to pray for those who confess their faults.

What is intended by faults in this text.

In this text, the word "faults" refers to such things as offenses against our neighbor or offenses against the public. Faults are also secretly besetting sins, or those secret lusts and temptations and states of mind that easily beset and frequently overcome us.

Offensive and injurious traits of character are also included here as faults. There are very few persons who have no features of their character that may be offensive, either to good morals or good social conduct, and are therefore injurious or even disastrous in their tendencies and results. These are different in nature to the above mentioned faults, but all such faults should be confessed one to another.

155

Such weaknesses and infirmities that lay us open to the power of temptation are faults. These weaknesses may be owing to some constitutional infirmity, or they may arise out of bad habits that have acquired great power over us. Whatever they are, if they are faults of a nature to bring us into legal bondage to sin, they doubtless come within the scope of the Apostle's meaning.

All such things as grieve the Spirit of God and hinder our growth in grace are faults.

To whom this confession is to be made.

Confession of faults is to be made especially to those who have been injured by our faults. That we are under obligation to confess to them, and make reparation if in our power, is too plain to need comment.

Public sins are to be confessed to the public. By this I mean, that if sins have been injurious to the public—to the Church, or to the world, or to both—the confession should be as public as the injury. But especially does this text require confession to our praying friends. "Confess your faults one to another," says the Apostle, "and pray one for another that ye may be healed." Although the duty of confessing sin to all that have been injured is abundantly taught in other parts of scripture; yet in this particular text, the Apostle obviously intended to enjoin the duty of confessing our faults to praying friends for the purpose of enlisting their sympathies and prayers in our behalf. And even more especially does he seem to require the duty of confessing our faults to eminently praying persons; for he immediately adds, "The effectual fervent prayer of a righteous man availeth much." Hence plainly, the Apostle intended to direct people to confess their faults especially to those who offer effectual fervent prayer.

The intention and purpose of confessing faults one to another.

The purpose of confessing our faults to one another is to make known to Christian friends our real circumstances and needs, so as to enlist their sympathies and enable them to pray for us intelligently, presenting our case before the Lord as it is. Without this knowledge, people may either altogether neglect to pray for us, or, if they pray at all, they may be in such ignorance of our real necessities as greatly to misconceive our needs, and therefore never benefit us by their prayers.

Another intent and purpose of confessing our faults one to another is to make reparation, so far as confession goes, for the wrong we have done. Until this is done, God will not forgive. For while we refuse to make the reparation within our power, it is not only unreasonable, but unjust, for God to pardon us.

To remove temptation to hard feelings on the part of those who have been injured by us is a value of confessing our faults. To injure a man by our faults is bad enough, but to refuse or neglect to confess is often worse, and may often result in worse consequences, and prove a greater injury to him, than did our original fault. If, after we have done wrong, and injured a brother or a neighbor, and he knows that we have done so, we persist in refusing to confess, it is a grievous temptation to him to entertain hard and revengeful feelings toward us. And where this course is persevered in, it often results in the greatest injury, if not in the absolute annihilation of the piety of the injured party. If, then, you have committed a fault, take the earliest opportunity to confess it, lest you lay a grievous or even fatal stumbling block at your brother's feet.

A further intent and purpose of confession is to remove obstacles to the restoration of Christian confidence and fellowship. When you have been guilty of a fault, and this is known to your brethren, they cannot and ought not to have Christian confidence in you, until you confess your faults to one another, and thus render Christian confidence possible.

Members of the same church may have little or no confidence in each other's piety. And whatever hope one may have that another is pious is founded not in the fact that he has any evidence that he is a Christian, but in the fact that he knows himself to be as poorly in things holy as the others, and is, therefore, constrained to hope for others on the same principle that he hopes for himself. In such cases there is not and ought not to be Christian confidence and fellowship. Nor ought there to be any hope among those who are Christians. For until they confess their faults one to another, and can heartily pray one for another, they are as far as possible from having any evidence that they are the disciples of Christ. Now the only possible way in which Christian confidence and fellowship can be restored in such cases is honestly and freely to confess your faults one to another.

Nothing is more calculated to beget sympathy, Christian compassion, and brotherly love, to draw out the heart in fervent prayer, than to confess our faults and lay our hearts open to our friends and brethren.

Confession of faults will promote our own humility. Humility is a willingness to be known and estimated according to our real character. While we are unwilling to confess we have no humility at all. Nothing is more directly calculated to deepen, perpetuate, and perfect humility than a full and frequent confession of our faults.

Another purpose and benefit of confession is to promote our own watchfulness. The very fact of confessing our sins to one another has a strong tendency to put us on our guard against repeating them. And on this account confession is of great importance to us. Confession also promotes watchfulness over us by others. If we confess our faults to others, we call their attention to our faults, and easily besetting sins, and thereby lead them to notice our walk and conversation, and to watch over us with a greater degree of Christian faithfulness than they otherwise would.

Confession will also encourage Christian reproof and admonition from our brethren. If we do not confess our sins, but on the contrary show a disposition to conceal them, our brethren will perceive that we are proud. They then have reason to believe that we would take offense if they should reprove us. If, on the contrary, we open our hearts to our brethren, we invite and encourage their Christian watchfulness and reproof, and thereby greatly promote their faithfulness to us.

By this practice of confessing our faults to one another we promote self-examination in others. Few things have a stronger tendency to fasten conviction upon the mind of others than to go to them with a frank and full confession of our sins.

It is much like holding up a mirror in which the other is forced to behold himself. Under scarcely any other circumstances have I seen myself so utterly vile, as when people have been ingenuously confessing to me their sins. It has so strongly called my attention to the facts of my own life, as often to fill me with shame and repentance.

Another design and tendency of confessing is to impress others with the truth of the Christian faith. When ungodly people may overhear the frank and heart-broken confessions of Christians, they will no doubt be struck with the contrast between this spirit and the spirit of the world. They secretly, and sometimes openly will exclaim, "If they see themselves to be such great sinners, what am I?"

Further, through confession of faults is the assurance of spiritual healing. "If we confess our sins, He is faithful and just to forgive us our sins and to cleanse us from all unrighteousness." Confession is indispensable to forgiveness. "He that covereth his sins shall not prosper; but whoso confesseth and forsaketh them shall find mercy."

It is indispensable to a daily walk with God. If people, at a given moment, are brought into the light, and remembering their sins, do not confess them, nor ask the prayers and forgiveness of their brethren, they will undoubtedly and surely backslide. For in neglecting this duty, they will grieve the Spirit, harden their hearts, and immediately fall again under the power of sin.

We are under special obligation to pray for those who confess their faults.

By their confessions, we have become acquainted with their necessities and know what we should pray for respecting them. Light increases obligation, and peculiar light in regard to their necessities brings with it peculiar obligation. We are under special obligation to pray for them, because there is special encouragement to pray for those who are willing to confess their faults. We have express promises upon which we can fasten in praying for such people; especially when they not only confess but forsake their sins. "If we confess our sins, He is faithful and just to forgive us our sins, and to cleanse us from all unrighteousness . . . Whoso confesseth and forsaketh shall have mercy."

To pray for them will be especially beneficial for *us*, if we have indeed been injured by them. (1) It will reveal to us the real state of our feelings toward them. Let a person attempt to pray for another, and he will soon discover the real state of his heart in relation to that subject of prayer. (2) It will beget in us the spirit of forgiveness. We cannot pray that an individual may be forgiven, and be honest and sincere in this prayer, unless we honestly forgive him ourselves. And nothing is more highly calculated to beget in us a spirit of forgiveness than to be much employed in praying for the forgiveness of others, especially for the forgiveness of those who have injured us.

The duty of praying for those who confess their sins is expressly enjoined in the text, and therefore a special obligation exists to make them particular subjects of prayer.

We see from this interpretation of the text why so many are in bondage to sin. The fact is, they do not and will not confess their sins. They give too much regard to their own reputation to confess their faults; hence, they wear their galling chains and remain the miserable slaves of sin.

We see why there is so little Christian sympathy and love. As long as professing Christians remain so ignorant of each other's past, joys, sorrows, trials and besetting sins, there is no such foundation or reason for Christian sympathy and love as there might be and ought always to be among the followers of Christ. We sometimes see two Christians who are in the habit of confessing their faults to each other, and disclosing their own experience to each other, and praying one for the other. In all such cases, without exception, you see much Christian sympathy and brotherly love. Such a course of conduct as this is indispensable to Christian sympathy; and this ought to be universally understood by the Church.

This subject reminds us how very little humility there is in the world. As I have already said, humility consists in a willingness to be known and estimated according to our true character. The world does not want to be known according to its true character because it would be found overwhelmingly wanting. But while there is so little confession in the Church of God, how can there be much humility there, as an example to the world? And *why* is there so little humility in the Church?

If Christians would but begin and make thorough work of confession this would greatly promote their humility; but until they begin, cast away their pride, and address themselves in earnest to confessing their faults one to another, their pride will never be crucified or their humility perfected.

There is but very little confidence among professing Christians in each other's prayers. If there were, they would more frequently confess to their brethren and beg them to pray that they might be healed. It is often amazing to see how little confidence church people have in prayer! Perhaps, living as they do, professing Christians have no right to have confidence in each other's prayers—in fact, without utter presumption, it is impossible that they should. Professing Christians very generally know that their own prayers are not answered; that they live in such a manner as to have no right to expect an answer to their prayers; and from observation they perceive that other professing Christians, with very few exceptions, live as they themselves do. In this view of the subject, how is it possible for them to have confidence in each other's prayers to the extent of soliciting the prayers of their brethren? Occasionally, there will be a professing Christian who is regarded by other professing Christians, and by the Church in general, as one who prevails with God. To me it is truly remarkable that they do not resort to such persons to confess their sins and ask their prayers. This can be accounted for only upon the supposition that there is very little honest and earnest desire to get rid of sin among professing Christians! If they were really determined to rid themselves of sin, it does appear to me impossible that they should not request the prayers and counsels of those whom they regard as eminent Christians.

James Brainerd Taylor was, according to his own account of himself, in earnest to get rid of his sins. He believed it was possible and felt that it was indispensable to his usefulness as a minister. He gave himself up thoroughly to the work of getting rid of his sins; and, as was very natural and scriptural, went to those whom he considered eminently pious and praying persons. To them he opened his heart and solicited their prayers on his behalf that he might be healed. And, blessed be God, he *was* healed.

So, Christian, you also may be healed, if you will go and do likewise with as much honesty and earnestness as he did. The unfortunate fact is, most professing Christians prefer remaining in bondage to confessing that they are so. They wear a cloak over their chains, and their hands are manacled, fast bound in sin. The law in their members wars against the law in their mind, keeping them in a state of perpetual captivity, so that they gather their cloak of concealment even tighter around them, seeking to cover their loathsome servitude and detestable chains rather than to throw off the covering, confess their faults, and be healed. Oh professing Christian, what a miserable slave you are. Hold up your hands. Let us see if they are not bound. Lay aside your cloak. Are you not the bond-slave of Satan, of lust, of the world?

How shameful and lamentable that people regard their reputation more than they hate sin, and prefer concealment to humility, reputation to holiness, and the good opinion of their brethren to the favor of God. In a very few cases, after all, do they by such concealment secure any reputation for real piety. Although they are ashamed to confess, and do not confess what the difficulty is; yet, as a matter of fact, every discerning mind sees that there is some difficulty, that they are not spiritual, that they do not walk with God, that they do not prevail in prayer. So that, after all, they gain nothing—not even reputation—by their concealment.

And this is the folly of sin: A person under its dominion will think to cover it up. But while some particular form of it may be disguised, its existence in some form will be known from the spirit and temper of the person, in spite of himself.

Confession, to be of any avail, should be frank and full, so as to give our brethren as full a view of our real character and needs as possible; so that they may understand, as far as may be, the worst of our case, and know how to present it before the Lord. If individuals will only half-confess, they will find that such confessions will do no good, but only harden their hearts. You must fully confess, and cover up no essential feature of your sin, if you expect to be restored.

Few things are so helpful and important to us and to those against whom we have sinned, as to confess our faults to them. When difficulties have existed between brethren, nothing can restore permanent confidence but a full, thorough, hearty, mutual confession of faults, one to another, and praying one for another, that they may be healed and restored.

There are but very few professing Christians who seem to know, or believe, that there is any such thing as spiritual healing in this world. They seem to reason thus: "Of what use would it be for me to confess my sins, as I am continually sinning? Why should I trouble the brethren with a detail of my sins, for they are as constant as the flowing of the waters? Why should I make myself the loathing of the Church of God by continually confessing my sins? It will do no good. I shall continue to sin on as long as I live; and I may as well, therefore, groan under my chains and continue this infernal service till I die. As to ever being healed—so as to get away from my sins in this life, it is out of the question."

Now, I can see why all this is not very natural and reasonable, when based upon the supposition that Christians have no reason to expect, in this life, entire emancipation from the bondage of sin. But brother, sister, let me beseech you to be no longer deceived in this issue. Remember, Christ is faithful, who has expressly promised, that if you confess your sins, He will not only forgive you, but "cleanse you from all unrighteousness."

12

WEAKNESS OF HEART

"How weak is thine heart" (Ezekiel 16:30a).

In this text, the prophet is speaking of the Church in reference to her past history. He says nothing of the real piety of the different generations of the Church; but in view of all her backsliding and inconsistencies, he exclaims, "How weak is thine heart!"

In discussing this subject, I will show what is understood by the term *heart* in this text, clarify what is implied in *weakness of heart*, and mention some things that either cause or are evidences of a weak heart. I will also indicate the remedy for weakness of heart, and tell what is implied in strengthening the heart.

What is understood by the term heart.

The language is figurative of necessity. We have no language by which to represent states of the mind unless we use some analogy that exists between mental states and material things.

The term heart is used in a great variety of senses in the Bible. Sometimes it obviously means the conscience, sometimes the whole mind or soul. Whenever it is spoken of as a

165

state of mind that has moral character and as the foundation or fountain of moral exercises it must represent a voluntary state of mind. When it is thus used, it cannot mean any faculty of the mind, but the particular attitude of the will in relation to moral subjects.

There must be some analogy between the fleshly organ of the body, called the heart, and the heart of the mind. The bodily heart propels the blood and keeps up the vital action of the whole system. It is in this sense the center of organic life. Out of it flows, by the force of its own contractions, that vital current which sustains both organic and animal life.

The heart of the mind is a voluntary disposition or preference of the mind. It is a disposition in opposition to a single exercise. It consists in a permanent, though voluntary, attitude of the will in relation to God and spiritual objects. It is a ruling disposition, or preference, in such a sense as to be the fountain out of which, as it were, flow those individual volitions and exercises of mind that make up its moral history. Therefore, as the bodily heart sustains organic and animal life, and may be regarded as the fountain from which the vital current flows, so the mental heart, this ruling disposition or preference of which I have spoken, is the fountain from which obedience to God or spiritual life flows.

What is implied in weakness of heart.

Weakness of heart is not an opposite heart ruling preference or attitude of the will. This cannot be; for the heart consists in a *supreme* disposition and *ruling preference*. It is impossible that there should be two supreme and opposite dispositions or preferences in exercise at the same time.

Weakness of heart does not mean a divided heart. This also is impossible. Keep distinctly in mind that the spiritual or moral heart is a supreme disposition or ruling preference of the will, and it is, of course, impossible that this should be divided.

A weak heart is not a wicked heart in such a sense as to

be the cause of wicked thoughts, volitions, emotions or actions. This is not possible. A regenerate heart is a holy disposition, a holy ruling preference of the will. It is impossible, therefore, that a regenerate heart should be a wicked heart in such a sense as to be the cause of any sinful emotion or affection.

By a weak heart is meant that this ruling preference or disposition of the will has not, for the time being and under the present circumstances, such efficiency as to successfully resist temptation to specific sins. The regenerate heart is not the cause of the sin; but the sin is in spite of the regenerate heart. That is, temptation prevails and occasions specific exercises of the will not in accordance with the regenerate heart; but, in opposition to it. Just as a wife, who loves her husband with a supreme affection, may, by the force of temptation, be betrayed into an individual exercise or act that is inconsistent with the general state and supreme attitude of her will. Just as parents who love their children with the most intense and absorbing affection may, through the force of temptation, feel exceedingly provoked with them and for the time being exercise feelings that are entirely in contrast with the state of their hearts toward their children. Every parent, and perhaps every husband and wife, can testify that such facts may exist, whatever their philosophical explanation may be.

Some things that are evidences of a weak heart.

One evidence of a weak heart is when there is great constitutional susceptibility to temptation. When the heart or ruling disposition is vigorous and healthy, it is difficult to get the attention of the mind to those things that are inconsistent with it. Take, for example, the case of a young convert who has been intemperate.

While in the healthy exercise of his first love, he abhors the thoughts of his former companions, and will not allow the thought of alcohol to remain for a moment in his mind.

But, should he leave his first love, the tendencies of his constitution would soon resume their control over him. He might then be unable to resist temptation to intemperance if he should again come in contact with his old acquaintances, or within the smell of a bar room. The same would apply to the convert who has been licentious. In the healthy exercise of his first love, he would so abhor his former ways as not to allow licentious thoughts to occupy his mind for a moment. A prostitute might pass before him, at the very sight of whom his whole soul would recoil; and feelings of the utmost disgust and loathing would surface. But should he leave his first love, his abused constitution would become so susceptible to the influence of temptation as might very probably cause him to fall.

Let it be understood, then, that when there is a great constitutional susceptibility to temptation, when artificial or constitutional appetites and passions are easily awakened, and the mind easily thrown into a state of turmoil in the presence of temptation, it is a sign of weakness of heart. The ruling disposition of the mind is not in a healthy and efficient state.

Another evidence of weakness of heart is a lack of firmness in the will whenever a temptation is presented to the mind. When the heart is strong, or the ruling preference in a healthy state, temptation cannot prevail because of the great and almost invincible firmness of the will. Thus, should a temptation to conjugal infidelity be laid before a young bride, when in the healthy and energetic exercise of deep affection for her husband, she might sooner submit to be murdered than consent to the embraces of another than her husband. But in the weakness of her heart, had she little or no affection for her husband, there might be such an utter lack of firmness in her will as greatly to expose her to seduction. Just so in the case of a young convert. In the healthy exercise of his first love, he might sooner suffer martyrdom than consent to sin. But should his heart become weak, should he leave his first love, no such firmness and stability of preference would remain to overcome and put down temptation. But on the contrary, whenever his emotions became excited by the proximity of some tempting object, he would find there was no firmness and strength of resolution in his will to resist temptation.

When a temptation is presented, and you find it difficult to resolve against its indulgence, it is because of the weakness of your heart. Suppose a man who has been formerly intemperate, licentious or gluttonous, finds it, in the presence of temptation to the commission of any of these sins, difficult to resolve against indulgence. He may know that if his heart is regenerate at all, it is in a state of extreme weakness. If, as a matter of fact, he does not find it easy to promptly resolve against indulgence, and to carry out this resolution in corresponding action, it is because of the weakness of his heart.

When you find it difficult to pray honestly and earnestly against a particular temptation, it is because of the weakness of your heart; that is, assuming that your heart has been regenerated. It must be owing either to the wickedness or weakness of the heart, and it may be consistent with either. If the heart has not been regenerated, it is wicked, and would, of course, prevent an honest and earnest appeal at the throne of grace against temptation. But if it has been regenerated and has become weak, temptation may get such a hold of the mind as to render it difficult to pray with perfect honesty and great sincerity against a given temptation under circumstances of particular excitement.

When you find it difficult to divert attention from an object of temptation, it is because of the weakness of your heart. If the heart, or ruling disposition, is in a healthy or efficient state, the attention will be naturally and promptly diverted from a seductive object. But when you find it difficult to divert your attention, and find that, in fact, the object has gotten possession of your thoughts and your excited feelings are clamoring for indulgence, there is great weakness of heart and the most imminent peril. Escape for your life, or you fall.

When former resolutions are found to be of no avail in the presence of temptation, it is because of the weakness of the heart. No resolution can prevail to put down temptation, unless the resolution is supported at the time of the temptation by the healthy efficiency of the heart. If the resolution was made when the heart was strong and vigorous, it will be of no avail, unless its foundation remains firm. Thus, a resolution never to touch a drop of strong liquor might be made in the ardor of the young convert's first love; but should he leave his first love, his resolution would be as yielding as air in the presence of temptation. When, therefore, you find that your resolutions to resist sin, obey God, and lead a holy life are of no avail in the presence of temptation, it is certain either that your heart has never been regenerated, or that at present it has no efficiency and is extremely weak.

When temptation easily excites anger, selfish ambition, envy, pride, vanity, lust, or any other unholy emotion or affection, it is certain either that the heart has never been regenerated, or that it is extremely weak.

When in the presence of temptation, and under the force of agitated feelings, the soul loses its apprehension of the guilt and consequence of that sin to which it is tempted, the heart has either never been regenerated, or it is extremely weak. If, when the passions become aroused, or the appetite for food excited in the presence of some tempting dish, the mind finds it difficult to realize the great guilt of indulgence to passion or to gluttony, the heart must be either wholly unregenerate or in a state of great weakness.

Causes of weakness of heart.

Ignorance is one cause of a weak heart. Of course, the stability of any disposition of mind and its efficiency depends in a great measure upon the reasons presented to the conscience for its exercise. Without a true knowledge of God there can be no true love to Him, and our love for Him will not exceed our knowledge of Him. Our estimate of spiritual and divine things must depend upon our knowledge of them. Where, therefore, there is great ignorance of God and of divine things, there will be a proportionate instability and lack of efficiency in the ruling disposition of the heart and mind.

Unbelief is another source of weakness of heart.

God and the things of God are realities to our minds only in proportion to our faith. It is unreasonable, then, to expect any efficiency in the ruling preference or heart, unless faith is active and eternal things have become realities to the mind. The physical condition may be and often is a cause of great weakness of heart. Ill health in general may be expected to render the actions of the mind feeble.

But especially diseases of the brain, spinal marrow, or diseases located in or sensibly affecting any of those organs that strongly sympathize with the brain, will of course greatly disturb the healthy action of the mind, and not infrequently render the heart, or ruling preference, extremely weak. All improper indulgences weaken the heart just as they weaken the conscience. Everyone knows that to persist in anything to which the conscience is opposed, gradually weakens it until it entirely, or in a great measure, is rendered inactive in respect to particular things. In like manner, any improper indulgence of appetite, passion, or undesirable exercise of mind whatever weakens the heart or the influence of the ruling disposition.

The remedy for weakness of heart.

Wait on the Lord: "Wait on the Lord: be of good courage, and he shall strengthen thine heart: wait, I say, on the Lord" (Psalm 27:14). "But they that wait upon the Lord shall renew their strength; they shall mount up with wings as eagles; they shall run, and not be weary; and they shall walk, and not faint" (Isaiah 40:31). In these passages the remedy for a weak heart is explicitly pointed out by God himself.

"Waiting upon the Lord" does not imply sitting still in apathy and leaving God to strengthen your heart in His own time and way, irrespective of your own effort. Many people think themselves to be waiting upon the Lord, when actually they have given themselves up to floating upon the stream of life without any concern about whether they are holy or sinful. They profess to be waiting God's time. Neither does waiting upon the Lord imply a self-righteous attitude of prayer, and the use of means, with the idea that we shall in this way influence God or recommend ourselves to Him.

"Waiting upon the Lord" does imply giving ourselves up to prayer, waiting in a constant attitude of watchfulness and supplication before God. It implies perseverance in prayer and in the use of all the means of knowledge and grace that are essential to strengthening our hearts. It will include repentance and putting away of sins, confession and restitution in all cases of wrong. There will be great fervency of importunity and implicit faith in the promises of God. It will involve submission to the wisdom and will of God in respect to the time and manner in which we will receive an answer. There will be a willingness on our part to have Him make use of any means which He deems necessary to strengthen our hearts—loss of property, friends, health, life, or anything that is necessary to strengthen our hearts and make us holy.

What is involved in strengthening the heart.

Strengthening the heart involves an increase of knowledge. In order to strengthen our hearts, we need to know and thoroughly consider those truths which are calculated to wean us from sin and strengthen our will and purpose in the spiritual life.

It also involves an increase of faith. Strengthening the heart must necessarily depend upon an increase of faith. For faith is always the condition of true love to God and stability in His service. It is impossible for the mind to be brought under the influence of scriptural truths any further than they are believed.

To strengthen the heart involves an increase of love. Supreme love and a supreme disposition to serve God are the same thing. Therefore, a strengthening of the heart is an increase of love to God and His kingdom.

It will involve such an absorption of the mind in God as to break the power of temptation. What power could temptation have over a person if he envisioned himself at the solemn Judgment, or standing in the broad sunlight of God's countenance? In such circumstances, temptation would pass by him like the idle wind.

It involves too, such a swallowing up of the attention and affections in God as in a great measure to prevent the soul from being tempted. By this I do not mean that the mind cannot in such circumstances be tempted; but that it is more difficult for temptation to gain the attention of the mind. When the attention is so fixed and riveted in God, and therefore enlarged and strengthened, that soul may say, as Christ did, "The prince of this world cometh but hath nothing in me"; no unsubdued lust, passion, or appetite remains, upon which to fasten a temptation.

A great many people have a very weak heart, who are not at all aware of it, simply because they make very little or no effort to resist sin. Making no effort to resist, they of course do not know how weak they would find themselves should they attempt to resist. They are literally "led captive by Satan at his will," and of course have no idea of the weakness of their hearts.

Many are aware of their weakness, but make no other than legal efforts to escape. They are trying to resist sin by resolutions and promises and struggling in their own strength. They do not seem to know that unless their heart is strengthened, all their resolutions founded upon legal considerations will be as yielding as air. They are convicted of sin—distressed, ashamed and agonized, sometimes almost despairing—and then they encourage themselves again by resolving and renewing their resolutions and binding themselves by solemn oaths and promises. But this is all to no purpose, for they are not supported by the active exercise of a supreme love to God. Their flesh will therefore be too strong for resolutions not founded in this love.

Others err by going to the opposite extreme. They do not depend upon legal efforts, nor indeed do they make any effort at all. But in typical Antinomian security, they settle down in an apathy which they call peace, and thus tempt Christ. They call that "faith" when they presumptuously throw upon Christ the responsibility of keeping them in such a sense as to exclude the active exercise of their own will.

The providence of God is designed to allow the development of a weak heart in His people, that they may see how much they are dependent upon His grace to strengthen them. Often individuals suppose that their sins are gone and that they have really overcome forever certain temptations. In this state, they are apt to forget that the ruling power of former habits is suspended only by the continual mercy and grace of God. If you forget that you are kept only by the power of God, He will in His providence soon show you again your weakness, and teach you to your sorrow and shame that your enemies are not dead, temptation is possible, and you cannot keep yourself. You are kept by the power of the Holy Spirit.

From these lessons we can see why Paul took pleasure in infirmities. It was so that the power of Christ might rest upon him: "And lest I should be exalted above measure through the abundance of the revelations, there was given to me a thorn in the flesh, the messenger of Satan to buffet me, lest I should be exalted above measure. For this thing I besought the Lord thrice, that it might depart from me. And He said unto me, My grace is sufficient for thee: for my strength is made perfect in weakness. Most gladly therefore will I rather glory in my infirmities, that the power of Christ may rest upon me. Therefore I take pleasure in infirmities, in reproaches, in necessities, in persecutions, in distresses for

Christ's sake: for when I am weak, then am I strong" (2 Corinthians 12:7–10).

Here Paul discovered the fact that his infirmities, that is, his weaknesses, emptied him of self-dependence. This brought him to put Christ in place of his resolutions. So that, instead of depending upon his own efforts and good intentions, he depended upon Christ.* Do you see what entire and permanent sanctification is? It consists in such a strength of heart as will resist all temptation to sin. Those who have a wicked heart are not born again.

A weak heart is not a wicked heart, as I have already explained. It is not the cause of wicked thoughts, emotions, and actions. A strong heart and a clean heart are not synonymous terms.

Whenever the heart is weak, the cause of this weakness, whatever it is, must, if possible, be put away. Sometimes the cause is physical, and such a state of the body renders the healthy operations of the mind impossible. But, in waiting upon the Lord to renew our strength, we must strive to do all that lies within us to put away the cause of the weakness of our heart. Whenever we have done this, and are waiting upon the Lord according to His directions, we are bound to exercise an unwavering confidence that He *will* strengthen our hearts. "Wait then, I say, on the Lord."

---

*For Finney's detailed exposition of how dependence upon Christ strengthens our hearts so we can overcome temptation and live the victorious Christian life of service, see his *Principles of Union with Christ*, a daily devotional on the names and titles of Jesus Christ and their practical application to us.

13

A SINGLE AND AN EVIL EYE

"The light of the body is the eye: if therefore thine eye be single, thy whole body shall be full of light. But if thine eye be evil, thy whole body shall be full of darkness. If therefore the light that is in thee be darkness, how great is that darkness!" (Matthew 6:22, 23).

In this discussion I will show what is implied in singleness of eye, what is implied in an evil eye, that singleness of eye will insure a knowledge of truth and duty, that an evil eye will insure darkness and delusion in regard to both doctrine and duty.

What is implied in singleness of eye.

This language is of course figurative. In speaking of a single and of an evil eye, we understand the Lord to be referring to a state of mind. "The light of the body," He says, "is the eye: if therefore thine eye be single, thy whole body shall be full of light." It is a matter of common knowledge that the weak eye will sometimes cause objects to appear double, and to obscure or give a false image which will naturally deceive or mislead the person. By a single eye, then, is meant an eye in its perfect state, when it sees objects as they are with such distinctness as to give the mind correct information. It also must refer to singleness of purpose and direction.

When this figure is applied to the mind, it must represent the supreme and ultimate intention of the mind. When the intention of the mind is single, and just as it ought to be, the eye of the mind may then be said to be single. For the mind has its eye upon but one great absorbing object. This state of mind implies supreme love to God. Of course, if the mind has but one great absorbing object or end in view, and that end is right, it must be to honor, please and glorify God. This certainly implies supreme love to God. It also implies disinterested love to Him—that is, God is loved for what He is, for His own sake, and not for the sake of making ourselves happy. If our own happiness is the end, the love and service of God is merely a means for the promotion of that end.

Singleness of eye is a state of entire consecration. We know that Christ intended "a single eye" to mean a state of entire consecration to God because of what follows the text. He says, "No man can serve two masters: for either he will hate the one, and love the other; or else he will hold to the one, and despise the other. Ye cannot serve God and mammon."

Plainly, the mind's eye is not right unless the soul is supremely and only devoted to the love and service of God. Nothing less than a state of entire consecration to God can be intended by a single eye.

What is intended by an evil eye.

An evil eye is that which has more than one object before it, or, it is seeing double. When this figure is applied to the mind, it means that state of mind in which objects are seen through a selfish medium, or when the mind has two objects in view, a legal intention to serve God, but an ultimate intention to serve self. By a legal intention to serve God, I do not mean that intention which is founded in supreme, disinterested love to God, which aims at honoring and glorifying Him as an ultimate end. But rather, it is an intention to serve God as the *means* of our own happiness, the end being self-interest, and the intention to serve God being a subordinate end.

Singleness of eye will insure a knowledge of truth and duty.

This is plainly taught in the text: "If thine eye be single, thy *whole* body shall be *full of light*." Light means knowledge, truth. Now when Christ says that your whole body shall be full of light if your eye be single, what else can He mean but that the soul that has a single eye shall be rightly instructed in all that is essential for it to know.

The natural result of singleness of eye will insure a knowledge of truth and duty because it will beget honest inquiry. It will be earnest and diligent in its search for truth. It will secure the right and the best use of the necessary means of knowledge. It will promote perseverance in the acquisition of knowledge. The state of the will, will not prevent the perception of truth and evidence. But the state of the will, will be such as to favor the perception, and insure the reception of evidence, when it is within its reach.

In this state of mind, the Spirit will not be resisted and quenched; but on the contrary, His influences will be sought and cherished. His instructions will be obeyed, His slightest inclinations heeded, and the whole soul will be delivered up to His guidance.

Being in the same state of mind in which God, and Christ, and the inspired writers were, a person with a single eye will naturally understand them. If you have the same end in view, and are in the same state of mind as God is, the language with which He expresses His mind will be most intelligible to you. Who does not know that people possessing the same spirit not only adopt the same or similar language to express their ideas and feelings, but naturally understand each other's language perfectly? To each other they are perfectly intelligible, while to those in a different state of mind, they are unintelligible in precise proportion to the diversity of their states of mind. Hence, the Bible is a very unintelligible and uninteresting book to an unrepentant sinner. Likewise, to a Christian of little experience, the Bible will be in a great measure unintelligible, and he may take little interest in it. To the Christian who lives in a state of entire consecration to God, the Bible is the most intelligible and interesting book in the world.

Whenever you are confronted with a subject in which you have experience, and in a manner and language that accords with your experience, you understand the speaker or writer with great ease and perfection. But in the degree to which he departs from your experience, he is unintelligible to you, in the same manner and for the same reason, as if he spoke to you in an unknown language. You do not understand language any further than it accords with your experience. Words are only signs of ideas. So that, when words are used which represent ideas not yet fixed in your mind, you do not comprehend the information.

The soul that lives in a state of entire consecration to God can come to Him with as much confidence, and with indescribably more assurance, than ever a child came to an earthly parent. And if you have ever been in this state, you know from your own experience. When you live all the time in deep communion with God, you also have a strong confidence that you know how He feels—know Christ's motives and feelings when He gave His life for sinners. You are conscious that you are willing yourself to make up in your body the sufferings that remain, and to lay down your life for the world and for the Church of God.

An evil eye will insure darkness and delusion in regard to doctrine and duty.

This is expressly taught in the text: "If thine eye be evil, thy whole body shall be *full* of darkness."

Imagine! The *whole* body shall be *full* of *darkness*. With such descriptive language as this the Savior must have intended to teach that a selfish mind would be full of error and delusion with regard to questions of doctrine and duty. A selfish mind, in this contect, refers to one that is not in a state of entire consecration to God; but is, rather, influenced by personal considerations.

Error and delusion will be the natural and inevitable result of this state of darkness, because selfishness will prevent inquiry—especially honest, diligent, and persevering inquiry. When the state of the will is directed by self, correct perception of truth is impossible, and reception of evidence is negligible. Few people seem to be aware of the extent of the influence of the will over the decisions of the understanding. I have for many years been in a situation to observe the developments of a mind in this respect; and have often been astonished to see to what extent the will influences human opinion. Almost everyone has observed that under circumstances of strong excitement, it is of little or no use to reason with a person against his prejudices. I have had repeated opportunities to observe, with pain, that prejudice of any kind on a matter will so influence the will as wholly to exclude the light of truth from the understanding. On many subjects, it seems next to impossible to convince a person, against his will; while, on the other hand, a person will believe almost anything which he is disposed to believe. The credulity of men on subjects that are in accord with the state of their will, and in regard to doctrines to which they are strongly disposed to believe, is as surprising as their incredulity upon subjects opposed to their will.

It is amazing to hear unbelievers and skeptics contend that human belief is involuntary, and that people necessarily believe what they do, when the self-will on any given opinion and belief is so striking and apparent to a considerate observer as almost any fact of the human story. A person with an evil eye, or a selfish heart, will not practice the truth, and therefore he cannot teach it. There are multitudes of truths which can be seen and understood no further than their face value. Other truths are never understood any further than they are experienced.

Take, for example, the subject of temperance. Suppose you preach strict temperance principles to a person who has always been in the habit of drinking alcohol freely. Now there are certain things which you can make him understand. If he has been a habitual drunkard, he can understand you when you describe to him the feelings of a drunkard; because upon this subject he has experience. Remember, words are signs of ideas; and to the drinker in this case, they will mean nothing more than the idea represented by the word in his mind. You can therefore make him understand something of the evil of drunkenness; and yet, if he has always been more or less intoxicated from his earliest recollection, you cannot in any language whatever so contrast his experience with that of a strictly temperate person, so as to make him understand you. He doesn't know what temperance is! He doesn't know what real health is. He is not at all acquainted with the state of mind which is the natural result of temperance and good health.

Now, if you can bring about conviction of the great evils of intemperance from the experience that he has on the subject, you could bring so much light upon his mind so as to break him of his habit. Then, gradually as he becomes a sober man, temperate and healthy, his experience will enable you to contrast temperance with intemperance so as to fully impress his mind with both sides of the question; and perhaps convince him of the momentous considerations in favor of temperance.

In all this process, it is easy to see that he must necessarily begin with the A, B, C's of both the facts and the experience of temperance. Break him of consuming hard liquor, and after a time he is better prepared to see and feel the indispensable necessity of universal temperance. Break him off from everything that intoxicates, and his experience will soon enable him to understand the importance and necessity of eliminating all non-nutritious stimulants in the diet. When he has abandoned all these, his experience will, in a little while, enable him to understand the importance of selecting the most wholesome and nutritious kinds of food.

The groundwork is then laid to prepare such a person's mind to understand the importance of overall cleanliness and chastity, the strictest subjection of the appetites and propensities to the great and universal law of temperance. And in short, as he goes from step to step in reform, and no further than he does so, he is in the circumstances to see, feel, understand and appreciate arguments in favor of further reformation.

Now what is true on the subject of temperance holds true on nearly every practical question; and especially is this true on subjects that pertain to moral holiness. If a man will not practice he cannot learn. Talk to an unrepentant sinner of entire sanctification. Holiness is so entirely opposite to his experience that he does not at all understand you. Talk with him about his sins and his convictions, his fears and misgivings, and any other subject that is a matter of experience with him, and on these subjects he will understand you. But talk to him of entire sanctification, and he has no idea what you mean. Therefore, the only possible way to deal with him is to begin with those subjects with which he has some experience, and bring him to see and to feel that it is an evil and disastrous thing to sin against God. This will lead him to see, admit and experience the necessity of repentance.

Now proceed, step by step, leading him forward; and as his experience enlarges, his capacity of understanding about sanctification, its desirability, its possibility will be perceived and felt by him. But no further than he practices can he properly learn. If he comes to a standstill and refuses to follow truth in daily practice, right there the clouds of darkness will descend about him. It is only as he goes forward, constantly progressing, practicing or experiencing each truth as it is presented, that he can possibly come to an understanding and knowledge of the truth. *Let it be a constant reminder that he who will not practice will not learn.* Unless the eye be single, the whole body will be full of darkness.

Selfishness *will* render the Scriptures unintelligible to him who has an evil eye. To him, the Bible is a sealed book. It is uninteresting, impractical, self-contradictory, irrelevant, anything but intelligible. The fact is, its Author and the inspired writers were in states of mind in direct opposition to selfishness. Therefore, to the evil eye, or selfish mind, they appear to be speaking in an unknown tongue. A selfish mind will not only find the Bible unintelligible, but in a great many instances will comprehend it as meaning the direct opposite of what it intends. The fault, of course, is not with the Bible, or its Author, but with the mind that is seeking to make sense of it from its selfish state.

For example, when God speaks of being angry with His enemies, since the sinner has never experienced anything but a selfish anger, he naturally understands God's anger to be like his own. In fact, when God speaks of any frame of mind, or action, or event, sinners naturally interpret His words by their own experience. So it is, as God says, "Thou thoughtest that I was altogether such a one as thyself." Interpreting, as they naturally do, the language of the Bible by their own level of experience, they ascribe the same motives, affections and passions to God, which they themselves have—not understanding that God's motives and actions are truly benevolent.

It is a familiar and true saying that people judge others by themselves. To a truly holy mind, the Bible is not only the most interesting, but also the most intelligible book in the world. While at the same time, unbelievers exclaim it is blasphemy to ascribe such feelings and conduct to God; and conclude, therefore, that the Bible must be a libel upon His character. Now for this there can be no remedy, unless one should become benevolent. If one should begin to obey the truth, so far as it can be understood, and practice one truth after another until he comes into the state of mind in which the inspired writers were, then, and only then will he understand the Bible.

In summary, a person who has an evil eye will not have the Spirit of God to enlighten his mind in regard to truth, and therefore, will never understand it.

Even a minister whose vision is limited to his own ends is a blind leader of the blind. This is the mildest language that truth or inspiration can use in regard to a selfishly ambitious, worldly minded, man-fearing, rather than God-fearing minister. His eye is evil. His whole body, as Scripture says, and thus his whole mind, is full of darkness on spiritual subjects. Such a minister will certainly in many things mislead his flock. He does not properly perceive spiritual truth, and therefore cannot safely be trusted as a spiritual guide. To trust him in these matters could lead to ruin and death.

Selfish minds are naturally willing to be led by selfish ministers, as they see eye to eye on many things. Having similar experiences they will easily understand each other. A carnal church will likewise be pleased with a carnal minister, and such a minister will not see the defects of such a church. They are truly able to walk together, because they are agreed.

The doctrine of the text applies also to the preparation and delivery of sermons. If a minister's eye is single he will naturally select those subjects of discourse that are suited to the condition of his people. He will naturally discuss them in a way and deliver them in a manner that will be edifying to the people, simply because that is the object at which he aims. Having his eye single to the holiness of the Church and the glory of God, it will be perfectly natural for him in the preparation and delivery of sermons to do everything in a manner that will tend to edify and sanctify the people. But if, on the contrary, his object is to secure his salary, play the orator, or promote any selfish interest whatever, he will contrarily select subjects, prepare, and deliver them in a manner suited to the end he has in view. If his eye is single, his whole mind will be full of light in regard to the manner of doing his work. If his eye is evil, his whole mind will be full of darkness, and he will do anything except edify and sanctify his people.

This doctrine applies to every decision made in every walk of life and with regard to any responsibility. In selecting a field of labor, course of life, a companion for life, or any other direction, if the eye is single, the whole mind will be full of light. Only those things will be taken into the account and carry weight that ought to influence the decision in question.

On the other hand, if the eye be evil, the whole body will be full of darkness; and the decision in question will certainly involve considerations that ought to have no influence on the outcome. If you are not conscious of a single eye, you cannot safely go forward in anything. If you have already made up your mind upon a question of doctrine or duty, and have not made it up under the influence of a single eye, you probably are entirely wrong. If in selecting a course of life, a field of labor, a kind of business, a location; if you have made a good bargain, or done anything else relating to the selection with a selfish intention, or under the influence of an evil eye, your whole body was full of darkness. The whole must be reviewed again to determine your motives and correct the errors in judgment.

Perhaps you are dismayed that many individuals seem very enlightened, hold good opinions, and are very orthodox, who are yet under the influence of selfishness. To this I answer both from my own experience and the Word of God: they hold the truth only in words. They know not what they say, nor whereof they affirm. They are deceived, and you are deceived in respect to them, if you think they know the truth. From this subject it is easy to see why the Church and the ministry are so divided in their opinions. It is because they are so sectarian and selfish in their spirit. It is selfishness, and nothing but selfishness, that divides the Church.

When the Church shall come to have a single eye, her watchmen and her members will then see eye to eye; because her body will then be full of light. You can also readily see the only way of promoting true Christian union. It is in vain to talk of destroying sectarianism by destroying creeds. Creeds may perpetuate, but they are not the cause of sectarianism. Selfishness, and nothing but selfishness, is its cause. Let universal love and a single eye prevail, and sectarianism is no more. Destroy a sectarian spirit, let it be supplanted by love, and Christians would then be in a state of mind to examine their differences of opinion with candor. After thoroughly and honestly weighing their thoughts and arguments they may discover that they almost coincide in opinion. But should there still be discrepancy of views in relation to any subject, it would be the farthest from their thoughts to withdraw from communion with each other and to divide into sects and separate denominations.

No wonder ministers who are not motivated from a single eye feel as if they cannot preach, have nothing to say and are at a loss to know on what subject to preach. No subject of Scripture has enough interest to them to enable them to preach on it. When they have fallen into a selfish state of mind their whole body is full of darkness.

How infinitely important it is that this truth should be continually remembered, that an evil eye, or selfish intention, invariably and necessarily brings the mind into great darkness. How many there are even in the Christian Church to whom the Bible is a sealed book, who are in great darkness in respect to truth, doctrine and duty; whose minds resemble an ocean of darkness.

How many there are, who have great confidence in their own opinions, who are ready to hazard their souls upon the truth of them, who have made up their minds on the most important and solemn subjects, while under the influence of selfishness. They have entered the Christian Church, but are clinging to their delusions, are following the guidance and instruction of those who are perhaps as much under the dominion of an evil eye as they are themselves, and whose mind is as full of darkness as their own. Thus they go on, unsuspectingly, while Christ assures them in the most solemn manner that if their eye is evil, their whole body is full of darkness. Still they will not believe it. They have the utmost confidence in their own opinions, and in the safety of their condition, and thus rush on, with a kind of insane assurance, to the depths of hell!

14

SALVATION ALWAYS CONDITIONAL

"Wherefore let him that thinketh he standeth take heed lest he fall" (1 Corinthians 10:12).

In remarking upon this subject I will show what is intended by one's thinking that he stands, in what such a confidence may be founded, that this confidence cannot secure the soul against falling into sin and hell, and that continued watchfulness and wakeful activity of soul are indispensable to continued holiness and final salvation.

What is intended by one's thinking that he stands.

The original word rendered *thinketh* in this text is used, according to some distinguished commentators, not to weaken but to strengthen the sense. In Luke 8:18, the same word is rendered *seemeth. Thinketh,* in this text, means great confidence, a strong assurance; as if the Apostle had said, "Let him that has great confidence, or a strong assurance that he stands, take heed lest he fall."

In what such a confidence may be founded.

A person may be very confident of his own good condition as a result of mistaken notions with respect to the natural

189

goodness of his character. He may even feel confidence that he shall persevere in holiness, perform all his Christian duty and be saved on the ground that he knows himself to be naturally able to obey God. This confidence may be founded in a dependence upon our own discretion, prudence, wisdom and zeal in the cause of Christ. It may be based upon confidence in our experience. Some are apt to rely very much indeed upon their own experience. They suppose themselves to be more than a match, even for the devil himself, in cases where they have the light of their own past experience to guide them.

This confidence may also be based on the consideration of what God has done for us; in the fact that He has so often given us grace to overcome temptation. Perhaps He has for weeks or months kept us in a state of perfect peace of mind, and we have been entirely exempt from any felt condemnation. A person may be very confident that he stands, because he believes himself to have been spiritually cleansed. He feels certain that God has renewed in him a clean heart and a right spirit; and from this he draws the assured conclusion that he shall not fall.

He may place great confidence in his purposed watchfulness. He feels so strong, and presently so steadfast in determination to watch unto prayer, and to pray in the Holy Spirit, that he feels strong to persevere in holiness. He may place great confidence in the strength of his own faith. Indeed, people are very apt, when in the exercise of strong faith, to suppose it next to impossible that they shall ever again be guilty of unbelief.

This is especially true if they are conscious, for a long time, of having exercised strong faith without any wavering. Further, confidence may be founded in the fact that we find ourselves to be dead to the influence of the world, and of the flesh, and, through grace, more than a match for the devil. When placed under circumstances in which we formerly found ourselves easily overcome, we may experience such a kind of supernatural strength, and find ourselves so lifted above the influence of temptation, so as to be confident that all our lust and sin is forever slain.

This confidence may also be founded in the promises of God. We feel that we believe them. We know it at the time, with as much certainty as we know that we exist, and hence infer and feel assured that God will keep us forever from falling under the power of temptation, and "preserve us faultless unto the coming of our Lord Jesus Christ."

This confidence, whatever may be its foundation, cannot of itself secure the soul against falling into sin and hell.

If this confidence is founded in anything naturally good in us, it is ill-founded of course, and cannot of itself secure our souls against falling into sin and hell. If it is founded in what grace has already done for us, it is ill-founded; for whatever grace may have done, it has not changed our nature. Our constitutional susceptibilities remain the same. It has not so changed our relationships and circumstances as to exempt us from temptation. Consequently, nothing that grace has done, or ever will do for us, can render our perseverance in holiness *unconditionally* certain.

If this confidence is based upon our purposed watchfulness, prayerfulness, experience, or faith; these, independent of the sovereign grace of God, afford no such foundation for our confidence as to render it at all certain, or even probable, that we shall not sin again. If this confidence is based upon the promises of God alone, it will not render our perseverance *unconditionally* certain. The promises of God are all conditioned upon our faith, and the right exercise of our own will. This is a revealed principle under the government of God. Look carefully at Ezekiel 18:21–29: "But if the wicked will turn from all his sins that he hath committed, and keep all my statutes, and do that which is lawful and right, he shall surely live, he shall not die. All his transgressions that he hath committed, they shall not be mentioned unto him: in his righteousness that he hath done he shall live. Have I any pleasure at all that the wicked should die? saith the Lord God; and not that he should return from his ways, and live? But when the righteous turneth away from his righteousness, and committeth iniquity, and doeth according to all the abominations that the wicked man doeth, shall he live? All his righteousness that he hath done shall not be mentioned: in his trespass that he hath trespassed, and in his sin that he hath sinned, in them shall he die. Yet ye say, The way of the Lord is not equal. Hear now, O house of Israel; Is not my way equal? Are not your ways unequal? When a righteous man turneth away from his righteousness, and committeth iniquity, and dieth in them; for his iniquity that he hath done shall he die. Again, when the wicked man turneth away from his wickedness that he hath committed, and doeth that which is lawful and right, he shall save his soul alive. Because he considereth, and turneth away from all his transgressions that he hath committed, he shall surely live, he shall not die. Yet saith the house of Israel, The way of the Lord is not equal. O house of Israel, are not my ways equal? are not your ways unequal?"

Look carefully at the context of Ezekiel 33:12–16: "Therefore, thou son of man, say unto the children of thy people, The righteousness of the righteous shall not deliver him in the day of his transgression: as for the wickedness of the wicked, he shall not fall thereby in the day that he turneth from his wickedness; neither shall the righteous be able to live for his righteousness in the day that he sinneth. When I shall say to the righteous, that he shall surely live; if he trust to his own righteousness and commit iniquity, all his righteousness shall not be remembered; but for his iniquity that he hath committed, he shall die for it. Again, when I say unto the wicked, Thou shalt surely die; if he turn from his sin, and do that which is lawful and right; if the wicked restore the pledge, give again that he hath robbed, walk in the statutes of life, without committing iniquity; he shall surely live, he shall not die. None of his sins that he hath committed shall be mentioned unto him; he hath done that which is lawful and right; he shall surely live."

Lastly, examine Jeremiah 18:7–10: "At what instant I shall speak concerning a nation, and concerning a kingdom, to pluck up, and to pull down, and to destroy it; if that nation, against whom I have pronounced, turn from their evil, I will repent of the evil that I thought to do unto them. And at what instant I shall speak concerning a nation, and concerning a kingdom, to build, and to plant it; if it do evil in my sight, that it obey not my voice, then I will repent of the good, wherewith I said I would benefit them." Any confidence in the promises of God, either for sanctification or final salvation, that does not recognize this universal principle in the government of God is ill-founded and vain; because God has revealed this as a universal principle of His government. Whether expressed or not, in connection with each promise, it is always implied. Overlooking this fact has often made the promises "a stone of stumbling" to those to whom they were given.

Continued watchfulness and wakeful activity of soul are indispensable to continued holiness and final salvation.

This is evident from the fact that moral government is a government of motives in opposition to a government of force. Moral beings are not and cannot be forced in the exercise of their moral choices. The motives of moral government are suited and addressed to the constitutional susceptibilities of moral agents. An analysis of the constitution of a moral being, as revealed to us by consciousness, will show that the motives calculated to influence moral agents may and must be divided into three classes: (1) Those addressed to hope or the desire of happiness. (2) Those addressed to fear or the dread of misery. (3) Those that move us to the exercise of disinterested love or benevolence.

Should we enter more particularly into this subject, these

classes of motives might be several times subdivided. But such subdivisions would carry me too far from my main purpose.

It is right to be influenced in a suitable degree or to a certain extent by each of these classes of motives. It is impossible that we should not be influenced to a certain extent by considerations that address our hopes and fears, if these considerations are apprehended by the mind. Selfish minds are influenced wholly by hope and fear; or in other words the motives that influence them to attempt obedience to God are purely legal; that is, those that are presented in the sanctions of the law of God. This state of mind is sin.

The three classes of motives which I have named, or those that address our hopes and fears, and those that move us to the exercise of disinterested benevolence, are indispensable to fill up the circle of moral influences. This is as certain as that the constitution of moral beings is susceptible to being influenced by these different classes of motives. We are conscious of possessing a nature adapted to the influence of these three classes of considerations. Unless, therefore, these three classes belong to moral government, and are indispensable to its perfection, moral government is not suited to the nature of moral beings.

The fact that conscience is a universal and indispensable attribute of moral agency demonstrates the universal and unalterable necessity of these three classes of motives. The Bible abundantly shows that neither the present sanctification, justification or final salvation of believers is so unconditionally decided as not to need warnings, threatenings, reproofs, and admonitions, and all those considerations belonging to these three great classes of motives.

God has shut up moral beings to a state of constant reliance upon Him for everything natural and spiritual. We are to depend upon Him for our daily bread. He does not send an ocean of waters upon the earth at once, but has shut us up to depend upon Him for rains in their season. He does not give food enough at once to last a man all his lifetime. His providence is such that, ordinarily, there is produced just about food enough for man and beast from year to year. In short, He so distributes His temporal favors as to make people see and feel their constant dependence upon Him.

This is equally true of spiritual blessings. He gives grace only from day to day, from hour to hour, and from moment to moment. He gives to no one a stock of grace upon which he can depend in the future without a constant reliance upon God, and a continual abiding in Christ. He deals with no one in spiritual things in such a manner that he can say to his soul, "Soul, you have many spiritual goods laid up in store for many years." But He has made continual reliance upon Christ indispensable to perseverance in holiness.

This course of procedure on the part of God, both in respect to natural and spiritual blessings, is naturally and unalterably indispensable to continued holiness. Suppose that God should cause food enough to grow in one year to last mankind a century; so that everyone could truthfully say, "I have much food laid up in store for many years." Would not such a procedure manifestly tend to a spirit of infidelity, to destroy a sense of dependence upon God, and beget among people a general forgetfulness and neglect of God? Who cannot see that should the arrangements of providence be such as to make people feel that all their temporal needs are already provided for, for a century, or for centuries to come, that it would ruin the world?

Just so in regard to spiritual things. If by regeneration, God really did, as some have supposed, change the very constitution of the soul, introduce, or implant within the soul, a holy principle that becomes a part of the constitution itself; in short, if He so remodeled the faculties, or made any such constitutional change whatever, as to beget the impression that the constant indwelling, abiding influences of the Holy Spirit are not essential to continued holiness, it would of course be the cause of universal backsliding and alienation from God. It is, therefore, indispensable to continued holiness that the mind should be shut up to a state of constant reliance upon the grace of God. And nothing can be more absurd, fanatical or dangerous than the idea that our perseverance in holiness, or final salvation, can be rendered *unconditionally certain.* It is naturally impossible for God to create a being who can be for one moment independent of Him. In Him all beings must "live, and move, and have their being."

To the fact that neither justification, sanctification nor final salvation can be unconditionally secured in this life by any act of ours or by any grace received; and that, therefore, continual watchfulness, godly fear, and a feeling of utter dependence are indispensable to continued holiness, some object that "perfect love casteth out fear."

To this I answer:

(1) This cannot mean every kind and degree of fear; for a certain kind and degree of fear is universally insisted on, not only as a duty, but as constituting an essential element of holiness.

Read carefully Psalm 111:10a: "The fear of the Lord is the beginning of wisdom." See also, 2 Corinthians 7:1b: "Let us cleanse ourselves from all filthiness of the flesh and spirit, perfecting holiness in the *fear* of God." Other uses of the term *fear* are found in: Ephesians 5:21: "Submitting yourselves one to another in the *fear* of God"; Psalm 2:11: "Serve the Lord with *fear*, and rejoice with trembling"; Matthew 28:8: "And they departed quickly from the sepulchre with *fear* and great joy . . ."; Philippians 2:12b: "Work out your own salvation with *fear* and trembling"; Genesis 22:12a: "And he said, Lay not thine hand upon the lad, neither do thou any thing unto him: for now I know that thou *fearest* God"; Psalm 112:1b: "Blessed is the man that *feareth* the Lord, that delighteth greatly in His commandments"; Psalm 128:1: "Blessed is every one that *feareth* the Lord; that walketh in His ways"; Proverbs 28:14: "Happy is the man that *feareth* alway: but he that hardeneth his heart shall fall into mischief"; Colossians 3:22: "Servants, obey in all things your masters according to the flesh; not with eyeservice, as menpleasers; but in singleness of heart, *fearing* God"; 1 Peter 1:17: "And if ye call on the Father, who without respect of persons judgeth according to every man's work, pass the time our your sojourning here in *fear*"; Hebrews 12:28: "Wherefore we receiving a kingdom which cannot be moved, let us have grace, whereby we may serve God acceptably, with reverence and godly *fear*."

(2) One of the characteristics of wicked people is that they do not *fear* God.

(3) Love casts out *slavish fear*, but not that kind of holy fear born of love, the foundation for the exercise of which is laid in the very constitution of our being.

Application

No one act of faith, nor any other exercise, can render salvation from sin or hell unconditionally certain. This is obvious from the fact that warnings and threatenings are addressed to the saints; which would be absurd if their justification or sanctification were already unconditionally certain. It is a principal mistake, and a dangerous error, to maintain that one act of faith brings the soul into a state of unconditional and permanent justification. That this view of justification cannot be true is evident from the following considerations:

(1) If the believer is so justified as not to come under condemnation if he sins, it must be because the law of God is abrogated. Some have maintained that the penalty of the law is forever set aside in his case, on the exercise of the first act of faith.

Now if this is true, then, as it respects him, the law is in fact abrogated; for a law without a penalty is no law. If the penalty is, as to him, forever set aside in such a sense that he may sin, and yet not be condemned and subject to that penalty, to him there is no law. The precept is only counsel or advice, as distinguished from law.

But if the law is set aside, he has no rule of action, no

obligatory standard of duty with which to compare himself. He can, therefore, be neither sinful nor holy anymore than the lost.

(2) That a believer is not unconditionally and permanently justified by any one act of faith is evident from the fact that every believer feels condemned in his own conscience when he sins. And if our own conscience, or heart, condemn us, is not God greater than our heart? Shall not He condemn us? "Shall mortal man be more just than God?"

(3) That believers are not unconditionally and permanently justified by one act of faith is plainly asserted in Ezekiel 18: 21–29, and 33:12–16, as quoted above. Nothing can be more to the point than these passages of Scripture. For here it is expressly affirmed that "if a righteous man forsake his righteousness, his former righteousness shall not be remembered"; but "in his sin that he sinneth shall he die."

To this some reply that these and similar passages are hypothetical, that they do not assert that any righteous man will fall from his righteousness; but only, that if he should, he would be condemned. However, I reply that this is the very thing for which I am contending. I admit that these and other kindred passages are hypothetical, and insist that for this very reason, they flatly contradict the proposition that by one act of faith believers are unalterably and unconditionally justified. They make the condition of continued justification to be continued obedience; and the condition of perfect justification to be perfect obedience.

(4) That one act of faith does not permanently and unconditionally justify the believer is evident from the fact already alluded to, that the Bible everywhere abounds with warnings, reproof, encouragements, and every possible inducement to perseverance in holiness to the end. Everywhere the Bible makes the condition of final salvation to be continuance or perseverance in holiness to the end of life.

Some object that these threatenings, warnings, etc., are the means by which the saints are caused to persevere in holiness. Yes, truly, I answer, so they are! And this very fact proves that they are not unconditionally or permanently justified, and that they are justified no further than they are sanctified. For what could all these warnings and threatenings amount to? Why should they be recorded? What possible influence could they have, upon the supposition that people are already perfectly, permanently, and unconditionally justified, and that, therefore, their final perseverance and final salvation are already unconditionally secure? Indeed, it is absurd to say that by one act of faith they have become unalterably justified, and yet, that only upon certain conditions, viz: their persevering to the end, can they be saved.

(5) That believers are not by one act of faith brought into a state of permanent or unconditional justification is evident from the manifest tendency of such a sentiment—this being the assertion in its most objectionable form, that if a person is once converted he will be saved, however much he may backslide, and even if he should die in this state of backsliding.

The certain knowledge and belief of unconditional salvation from sin, or hell, or of unconditional justification and salvation would break the power of moral government and insure a fall. It would destroy the balance of motives and nullify entirely the power of that class of motives that are addressed to the hopes and fears of people. What, I pray you, would all the warnings of the Bible avail to sustain the virtue of a person, who already knew himself to be in a state of unconditional salvation from sin, condemnation and hell? Do you answer that he does not need them, and that all regard to them would be selfishness? I ask, why then are they found in the Bible actually and everywhere addressed to the saints?

To this some may reply that a sanctified soul is influenced by love, and not at all by hope and fear. I answer that this is true, that love is the mainspring of action. But it is also true that both the hopes and fears of people sustain such a relation to moral government, and that admonitions addressed to them make up an indispensable part of those influences that sustain the soul in a course of steady obedience. To this it is objected again that those saints who have believed themselves to be in a state of unconditional justification, and who have had the felt assurance of their final perseverance and salvation have not found that this felt assurance was a stumbling block to them, but have felt sustained in virtue by this very consideration. To this I answer that if by the faith of assurance is meant our assurance of final perseverance in holiness, and consequent salvation, I can easily see that such an assurance would not be a stumbling block to the soul. But, notice, this is not an assurance of unconditional justification.

For saints who have this assurance have universally believed that their justification and salvation were conditioned upon their continued holiness. They have believed that if they fall into sin, they are condemned, and that, should they die in their sins, or in a backslidden state, they would be damned. Their belief and assurance have been that they should, through grace assisting them, be enabled so to exercise faith and persevere in the use of their powers of moral agency as to be finally justified and saved.

This assurance is eminently calculated to encourage them in all ways of well-doing, and in the most strenuous efforts to perfect holiness in the fear of God. But suppose they get the idea that they have so believed in Christ as to render their continued holiness, their permanent justification and final salvation, unconditionally certain: this is an eminently dangerous and ruinous belief, and is as far as possible from any state of mind encouraged by the Word of God.

Moral beings cannot be in a state of unconditional sanctification or justification in any world. This is evident from the fact that they cannot be put beyond the natural possibility of sinning. If they were, they would be put beyond the possibility of being holy. Holiness implies moral liberty. Moral liberty implies the power of doing right or wrong. It is, therefore, naturally impossible that moral beings should in any world be placed under circumstances where their eternal justification, sanctification and salvation are unconditionally certain. The continued justification of the inhabitants of heaven must be forever conditioned upon their continued holiness. And their continued holiness must ever depend upon and consist in the right voluntary exercise of their powers of moral agency. And nothing but that grace which is perfectly consistent with the exercise of their own liberty can render their final perseverance certain.

"Fearing always," or "passing the time of our sojourning here with fear," as the Apostle commands, does not imply unbelief, and is not a sinful state of mind; because the promises of God are all conditional. Since the promises of sanctification are conditioned upon our own faith, and the promises of justification conditioned upon our sanctification, and as all is suspended upon the right use of the powers of moral agency which we possess, it behooves us to "fear always—to walk softly, to gird up the loins of our minds, to be sober, vigilant, and to run with patience the race set before us."

The assurance that we shall never sin again does not secure us against sin, and has in this world of severe temptation an obvious tendency to procure our fall. Nor does a fall, in such a case, in the least degree tend to prove that there is no such state as that of permanent sanctification in this life. Nor does it impeach the veracity of Christ. Some people have supposed that they have attained a state of permanent sanctification, and felt assured that they should never sin again. They have maintained that the veracity of Christ was pled   ⅃ in such a sense that He would be guilty of falsehood if He should allow them to fall into sin. They seem to have inferred this from the fact that a promise of Christ's keeping power had been deeply impressed upon their minds. Afterwards, however, they have fallen into sin, and have been greatly tempted to entertain bitter thoughts toward Christ, to impeach His veracity, and deny His truth.

Now the mistake in this case was in overlooking the fact that all the promises of Christ are from their very nature conditioned upon the continued exercise of faith by us. Misunderstanding the promise, and leaving out of view the condition, was the foundation of the assumption that Christ was pledged for their perseverance in holiness; and if they have fallen into sin the blame is their own. Some have expected of Christ what He has never promised, except upon a condition that these same have not fulfilled.

To this view of the subject it has been objected that if this is true, the promises of the gospel amount only to this, that *Christ will keep us if we will keep ourselves.* To this I answer:

(1) In a very important sense, this is true. I formerly felt the same objection myself, and was strongly inclined to, and even entertained an opposite opinion. What, I said, can the promises of the gospel mean more than this: "I will keep him who will keep himself?" Much consideration and prayer, with searching the Word of God, have led me to the conviction that this is the exact truth, and this opinion is in exact keeping with the whole providential government of God.

(2) Take, for example, all temporal blessings. Who does not know that all the promises of daily bread are so conditioned upon the use of indispensable means, that they amount to this: "I will feed him who will feed himself; I will take care of him who will take care of himself." Take all the promises that respect the things of this life, and the same will be found to be true. If God promises health, it is upon the condition that we obey the laws of our physical being; so that the promise amounts to this, "I will keep him in health who will keep himself in health." If He promises to prolong our natural life, it is upon condition that we comply with the indispensable laws of life, so that the promise amounts to this, "I will keep him alive who will keep himself alive."

Now the same is emphatically and eminently true of all spiritual blessings. Who does not know for a fact that every believer progresses in his Christian walk precisely in proportion to his own faithfulness; that God keeps him from falling when he watches and thereby keeps himself from falling; that he has the spirit of prayer in proportion as he watches unto prayer and prays in the Holy Spirit; and that, as a matter of fact, He keeps the saints only through their own watchfulness, faithfulness and efforts, so that it may be truly said that He keeps those only who will keep themselves; that He saves those only who will save themselves. Nor does this in the least degree set aside or depreciate the grace of God; nor at all deny or set aside any correct idea of the sovereignty of God. Who ever supposed that the farmer, who tills his land, the mechanic, who plies his trade, or the student, who trims his midnight lamp, either denies or sets aside the sovereignty of God in accomplishing the ends at which he aims? Indeed, the sovereignty of God consists in this, in bringing about the great ends of His government through the agency of His creatures; and no correct idea of His sovereignty will ever leave out of view the use of the natural and indispensable means of procuring the things which He has promised.

Nor does this view of the subject at all touch the question of the perseverance of the saints, as I understand that doctrine to be taught in the Bible. The doctrine there inculcated, if I understand it, is not that by one act of faith people are brought into a state of unconditional and unalterable justification; but that the saints, through the grace of God, will be kept in ways of obedience to the end.

Although there can be no unconditional certainty of perpetual holiness, justification or final salvation, in any world, yet we can have such a kind of assurance of all these as to cast out all slavish fear that has torment. Do you not think that the angels know and saints in heaven know that if they should sin, they would be sent to hell? And think you not that they know they have power to sin, are liable to sin, and that without watchfulness and wakeful activity and perseverance, they will sin? They must know this; and yet, this knowledge does not bring them into slavish bondage, but affords just that healthy and holy stimulus to holy perseverance that is demanded by the very constitution of moral agency in any world.

Sanctification, justification and final salvation are all

based on the same ground. It cannot be true that people are justified any further than they are sanctified; or that they are or ever can be saved any further than they are cleansed from sin. Gospel justification is generally defined to be pardon and acceptance. But can a person be pardoned any further than he is penitent? Can the soul be accepted any further than it is obedient? Certainly it cannot be, unless Antinomianism is true and the law of God is abrogated. The distinction, then, that is commonly made (which I, following the trends of the Church without sufficient examination, once held myself) between instantaneous justification and progressive sanctification must be without foundation. Everyone feels that he is condemned, and not justified, when he sins, and that he is kept out of condemnation only by keeping out of sin. This is the doctrine of the Bible. It is the doctrine of conscience and of common sense. And it is certainly a most licentious view of the doctrine of justification that maintains that justification is perfected while sanctification is imperfect; that justification is instantaneous, while sanctification is progressive.

Beloved Christian, why do you pray for forgiveness when you sin? Is it not because you feel condemned? But if you were already perfectly and permanently justified, you are mistaken in praying for forgiveness; for you are already forgiven, and not condemned. You cannot possibly be pardoned, unless you are condemned; for what is pardon, but setting aside the execution of law? If, therefore, people are permanently justified by one act of faith, they not only have no need of pardon from that moment on, however much they may sin, but to pardon them is impossible, since they are not condemned. And why, let me ask you, should Christ teach you to pray daily for the forgiveness of your sins, if by one act of faith you are permanently justified? Let me conclude, then, by saying, "Let him that thinketh he standeth, take heed lest he fall."

EDITOR'S NOTE

The lectures in this book originally appeared in *The Oberlin Evangelist* in 1840, and follow Finney's nine lectures on sanctification, published as *Principles of Sanctification*. *Principles of Christian Obedience* completes the publication of Finney's sermons and lectures from the 1840 issues of *The Oberlin Evangelist*.

One of the lectures, "Death to Sin," published in the July 15, 1840, issue of *The Oberlin Evangelist*, was retitled "The Nature of Death" and published in *Principles of Liberty*, because it was a lecture on Romans. For this reason, it is not reprinted in *Principles of Christian Obedience*. If it had been incorporated here, it would have followed Chapter 4, "A Willing Mind, Indispensable to a Right Understanding of Truth."

Following is a listing of the chapter numbers in *Principles of Christian Obedience* along with their date of publication in *The Oberlin Evangelist* newspaper.

1. May 6, 1840.
2. May 20, 1840.
3. June 3, 1840.
4. July 1, 1840.
5. July 29, 1840.

   6. August 12, 1840.

   7. August 26, 1840.

   8. September 2, 1840.

   9. October 7, 1840.

  10. October 21, 1840.

  11. November 4, 1840.

  12. November 18, 1840.

  13. December 2, 1840.

  14. December 16, 1840.

Lectures and sermons not previously published in the "Principles Series" from the years 1841–42, will be published as *Principles of Consecration*. Sermons from 1843 are published in *Principles of Holiness*.